ABOUT THIS PUBLICATION

FOR SERVICE ASSISTANCE

Customer Service Department
704.898.0770

North Carolina General Statues is published by The Muliti-Media Group of Greater Charlotte in Charlotte, North Carolina. Copyright 2015 by the Multi-Media Group of Greater Charlotte. This book or parts thereof may not be reproduced in any form, stored in a retrieval system, or transmitted in any form by any means—electronic, mechanical, photocopy, recording or otherwise—without prior written permission of the publisher, except as provided by United States of America copyright law.

The records required by U.S. Code 2257(a) through (c) and the pertinent regulations 28 C.F.R. Cli. 1, Part 75 with respect to this publication and all materials associated with such records are maintained by The Multi-Media Group of Greater Charlotte, Publisher and available for review by Attorney General.

www.visionbooks.org

Copyright © 2015 by MMGGC
All rights reserved!

TID: 5015290
ISBN (10) digit: 1502485176
ISBN (13) digit: 978-1502485175

123-4-56789-01234-Paperback
123-4-56789-01234-Hardback

First Edition

090520140547

Printed in the United States of America

2015 EDITION

North Carolina Criminal Law And Procedure-Pamphlet # 16

Printed In conjunction with the Administration of the Courts

North Carolina Criminal Law and Procedure
Pamphlet Reference Guide

Chapters	Pamphlet
Chapter 1 Civil Procedure	1
Chapter 1 Civil Procedure (Continue)	2
Chapter 1A Rules of Civil Procedure	2
Chapter 1B Contribution.	2
Chapter 1C Enforcement of Judgments.	2
Chapter 1D Punitive Damages.	2
Chapter 1E Eastern Band of Cherokee Indians.	2
Chapter 1F North Carolina Uniform Interstate Depositions and Discovery Act.	2
Chapter 2 - Clerk of Superior Court [Repealed and Transferred.]	3
Chapter 3 - Commissioners of Affidavits and Deeds [Repealed.]	3
Chapter 4 - Common Law	3
Chapter 5 - Contempt [Repealed.]	3
Chapter 5A - Contempt	3
Chapter 6 - Liability for Court Costs	3
Chapter 7 - Courts [Repealed and Transferred.]	3
Chapter 7A – Judicial Department	3
Chapter 7A – Continuation (Judicial Department)	4
Chapter 7A – Continuation (Judicial Department)	5
Chapter 7B - Juvenile Code	5
Chapter 8 - Evidence	6
Chapter 8A - Interpreters for Deaf Persons [Recodified.]	6
Chapter 8B - Interpreters for Deaf Persons	6
Chapter 8C - Evidence Code	6
Chapter 9 - Jurors	6
Chapter 10 - Notaries [Repealed.]	6
Chapter 10A - Notaries [Recodified.]	6
Chapter 10B - Notaries	6
Chapter 11 - Oaths	6
Chapter 12 - Statutory Construction	6
Chapter 13 - Citizenship Restored	6
Chapter 14 - Criminal Law	7
Chapter 14 –Criminal Law (Continuation)	8
Chapter 15 - Criminal Procedure	9
Chapter 15A - Criminal Procedure Act (Continuation)	10
Chapter 15A - Criminal Procedure Act (Continuation)	11
Chapter 15B - Victims Compensation	11
Chapter 15C - Address Confidentiality Program	11
Chapter 16 - Gaming Contracts and Futures	11
Chapter 17 - Habeas Corpus	11

Chapter 17A - Law-Enforcement Officers [Recodified.]	11
Chapter 17B - North Carolina Criminal Justice Education and Training System [Recodified.] Chapter 17C - North Carolina Criminal Justice Education and Training Standards Commission	11
	11
Chapter 17D - North Carolina Justice Academy	11
Chapter 17E - North Carolina Sheriffs' Education and Training Standards Commission	11
Chapter 18 - Regulation of Intoxicating Liquors [Repealed.]	12
Chapter 18A - Regulation of Intoxicating Liquors [Repealed.]	12
Chapter 18B - Regulation of Alcoholic Beverages	12
Chapter 18C - North Carolina State Lottery	12
Chapter 19 - Offenses against Public Morals	12
Chapter 19A - Protection of Animals	12
Chapter 20 - Motor Vehicles	13
Chapter 20 - Motor Vehicles (Continuation)	14
Chapter 20 - Motor Vehicles (Continuation)	15
Chapter 20 - Motor Vehicles (Continuation)	16
Chapter 21 - Bills of Lading	17
Chapter 22 - Contracts Requiring Writing	17
Chapter 22A - Signatures	17
Chapter 22B - Contracts Against Public Policy	17
Chapter 22C - Payments to Subcontractors	17
Chapter 23 - Debtor and Creditor	17
Chapter 24 – Interest	17
Chapter 25 – Uniform Commercial Code	18
Chapter 25 – Uniform Commercial Code (Continuation)	19
Chapter 25A – Retail Installment Sales Act	20
Chapter 25B - Credit	20
Chapter 25C - Sales of Artwork	20
Chapter 26 - Suretyship	20
Chapter 27 - Warehouse Receipts [Repealed.]	20
Chapter 28 - Administration [Repealed.]	20
Chapter 28A - Administration of Decedents' Estates	20
Chapter 28B - Estates of Absentees in Military Service	20
Chapter 28C - Estates of Missing Persons	20
Chapter 29 - Intestate Succession	21
Chapter 30 - Surviving Spouses	21
Chapter 31 - Wills	21
Chapter 31A - Acts Barring Property Rights	21
Chapter 31B - Renunciation of Property and Renunciation of Fiduciary Powers Act	21
Chapter 31C - Uniform Disposition of Community Property Rights at Death Act	21
Chapter 32 - Fiduciaries	21
Chapter 32A - Powers of Attorney	21
Chapter 33 - Guardian and Ward [Repealed and Recodified.]	21

Chapter 33A - North Carolina Uniform Transfers to Minors Act	21
Chapter 33B - North Carolina Uniform Custodial Trust Act	21
Chapter 34 - Veterans' Guardianship Act	22
Chapter 35 - Sterilization Procedures	22
Chapter 35A - Incompetency and Guardianship	22
Chapter 36 - Trusts and Trustees [Repealed.]	22
Chapter 36A - Trusts and Trustees	22
Chapter 36B - Uniform Management of Institutional Funds Act [Repealed.]	22
Chapter 36C - North Carolina Uniform Trust Code	22
Chapter 36D - North Carolina Community Third Party Trusts, Pooled Trusts	23
Chapter 36E - Uniform Prudent Management of Institutional Funds Act	23
Chapter 37 - Allocation of Principal and Income [Repealed.]	23
Chapter 37A - Uniform Principal and Income Act	23
Chapter 38 - Boundaries	23
Chapter 38A - Landowner Liability	23
Chapter 39 - Conveyances	23
Chapter 39A - Transfer Fee Covenants Prohibited	23
Chapter 40 - Eminent Domain [Repealed.]	23
Chapter 40A - Eminent Domain	23
Chapter 41 - Estates	23
Chapter 41A - State Fair Housing Act	23
Chapter 42 - Landlord and Tenant	23
Chapter 42A - Vacation Rental Act	23
Chapter 43 - Land Registration	23
Chapter 44 - Liens	24
Chapter 44A - Statutory Liens and Charges	24
Chapter 45 - Mortgages and Deeds of Trust	24
Chapter 45A - Good Funds Settlement Act	24
Chapter 46 - Partition	24
Chapter 47 - Probate and Registration	25
Chapter 47A - Unit Ownership	25
Chapter 47B - Real Property Marketable Title Act	25
Chapter 47C - North Carolina Condominium Act	25
Chapter 47D - Notice of Settlement Act [Expired.]	25
Chapter 47E - Residential Property Disclosure Act	25
Chapter 47F - North Carolina Planned Community Act	25
Chapter 47G - Option to Purchase Contracts	25
Chapter 47H - Contracts for Deed	25
Chapter 48 - Adoptions +	26
Chapter 48A - Minors	26
Chapter 49 - Bastardy	26
Chapter 49A - Rights of Children	26
Chapter 50 - Divorce and Alimony	26
Chapter 50A - Uniform Child-Custody Jurisdiction and	

Enforcement Act	26
Chapter 50B - Domestic Violence	26
Chapter 50C - Civil No-Contact Orders	26
Chapter 51 - Marriage	26
Chapter 52 - Powers and Liabilities of Married Persons	27
Chapter 52A - Uniform Reciprocal Enforcement of Support Act [Repealed.]	27
Chapter 52B - Uniform Premarital Agreement Act	27
Chapter 52C - Uniform Interstate Family Support Act	27
Chapter 53 - Banks	27
Chapter 53A - Business Development Corporations and North Carolina Capital Resource Corporations	28
Chapter 53B - Financial Privacy Act	28
Chapter 54 - Cooperative Organizations	28
Chapter 54A - Capital Stock Savings and Loan Associations [Repealed.]	28
Chapter 54B - Savings and Loan Associations	29
Chapter 54C - Savings Banks	29
Chapter 55 - North Carolina Business Corporation Act	30
Chapter 55A - North Carolina Nonprofit Corporation Act	31
Chapter 55B - Professional Corporation Act	31
Chapter 55C - Foreign Trade Zones	31
Chapter 55D - Filings, Names, and Registered Agents for Corporations, Nonprofit Corporations, and Partnerships	31
Chapter 56 - Electric, Telegraph and Power Companies [Repealed.]	31
Chapter 57 - Hospital, Medical and Dental Service Corporations [Recodified.]	31
Chapter 57A - Health Maintenance Organization Act [Recodified.]	31
Chapter 57B - Health Maintenance Organization Act [Recodified.]	31
Chapter 57C - North Carolina Limited Liability Company Act.	31
Chapter 58 - Insurance.	32
Chapter 58 - Insurance (Continuation)	33
Chapter 58 - Insurance (Continuation)	34
Chapter 58 - Insurance (Continuation)	35
Chapter 58 - Insurance (Continuation)	36
Chapter 58 - Insurance (Continuation)	37
Chapter 58 - Insurance (Continuation)	38
Chapter 58A - North Carolina Health Insurance Trust Commission [Recodified.]	38
Chapter 59 - Partnership.	39
Chapter 59B - Uniform Unincorporated Nonprofit Association Act.	39
Chapter 60 - Railroads and Other Carriers [Repealed and Transferred.]	39
Chapter 61 - Religious Societies	39
Chapter 62 - Public Utilities	39

Chapter 62 - Public Utilities (Continuation)	40
Chapter 62A - Public Safety Telephone Service And Wireless Telephone Service	40
Chapter 63 - Aeronautics	40
Chapter 63A - North Carolina Global TransPark Authority	40
Chapter 64 - Aliens	40
Chapter 65 – Cemeteries	40
Chapter 66 - Commerce and Business	41
Chapter 67 - Dogs	41
Chapter 68 - Fences and Stock Law	41
Chapter 69 - Fire Protection	41
Chapter 70 - Indian Antiquities, Archaeological Resources and Unmarked Human Skeletal Remains Protection	42
Chapter 71 - Indians [Repealed.]	42
Chapter 71A - Indians	42
Chapter 72 - Inns, Hotels and Restaurants	42
Chapter 73 - Mills	42
Chapter 74 - Mines and Quarries	42
Chapter 74A - Company Police [Repealed.]	42
Chapter 74B - Private Protective Services Act [Repealed.]	42
Chapter 74C - Private Protective Services	42
Chapter 74D - Alarm Systems	42
Chapter 74E - Company Police Act	42
Chapter 74F - Locksmith Licensing Act	42
Chapter 74G - Campus Police Act	42
Chapter 75 - Monopolies, Trusts and Consumer Protection	42
Chapter 75A - Boating and Water Safety	43
Chapter 75B - Discrimination in Business	43
Chapter 75C - Motion Picture Fair Competition Act	43
Chapter 75D - Racketeer Influenced and Corrupt Organizations	43
Chapter 75E - Unlawful Activities in Connection With Certain Corporate Transactions	43
Chapter 76 - Navigation	43
Chapter 76A - Navigation and Pilotage Commissions	43
Chapter 77 - Rivers, Creeks, and Coastal Waters	43
Chapter 78 - Securities Law [Repealed.]	43
Chapter 78A - North Carolina Securities Act	43
Chapter 78B - Tender Offer Disclosure Act [Repealed.]	43
Chapter 78C - Investment Advisers	43
Chapter 78D - Commodities Act	43
Chapter 79 - Strays [Repealed.]	43
Chapter 80 - Trademarks, Brands, etc.	44
Chapter 81 - Weights and Measures [Recodified.]	44
Chapter 81A - Weights and Measures Act of 1975.	44
Chapter 82 - Wrecks [Repealed.]	44
Chapter 83 - Architects [Recodified.]	44

Chapter 83A - Architects	44
Chapter 84 - Attorneys-at-Law	44
Chapter 84A - Foreign Legal Consultants	44
Chapter 85 - Auctions and Auctioneers [Repealed.]	44
Chapter 85A - Bail Bondsmen and Runners [Recodified.]	44
Chapter 85B - Auctions and Auctioneers	44
Chapter 85C - Bail Bondsmen and Runners [Recodified.]	44
Chapter 86 - Barbers [Recodified.]	44
Chapter 86A - Barbers	44
Chapter 87 - Contractors	44
Chapter 88 - Cosmetic Art [Repealed.]	44
Chapter 88A - Electrolysis Practice Act	44
Chapter 88B - Cosmetic Art	45
Chapter 89 - Engineering and Land Surveying [Recodified.]	45
Chapter 89A - Landscape Architects	45
Chapter 89B - Foresters	45
Chapter 89C - Engineering and Land Surveying	45
Chapter 89D - Landscape Contractors	45
Chapter 89E - Geologists Licensing Act	45
Chapter 89F - North Carolina Soil Scientist Licensing Act	45
Chapter 89G - Irrigation Contractors	45
Chapter 90 - Medicine and Allied Occupations	45
Chapter 90 - Medicine and Allied Occupations (Continuation)	46
Chapter 90 - Medicine and Allied Occupations (Continuation)	47
Chapter 90 - Medicine and Allied Occupations (Continuation)	48
Chapter 90A - Sanitarians and Water and Wastewater Treatment Facility Operators	48
Chapter 90B - Social Worker Certification and Licensure Act	48
Chapter 90C - North Carolina Recreational Therapy Licensure Act	48
Chapter 90D - Interpreters and Transliterators	48
Chapter 91 - Pawnbrokers [Repealed.]	48
Chapter 91A - Pawnbrokers Modernization Act of 1989	48
Chapter 92 - Photographers [Deleted.]	48
Chapter 93 - Certified Public Accountants	48
Chapter 93A - Real Estate License Law	49
Chapter 93B - Occupational Licensing Boards	49
Chapter 93C - Watchmakers [Repealed.]	49
Chapter 93D - North Carolina State Hearing Aid Dealers and Fitters Board.	49
Chapter 93E - North Carolina Appraisers Act	49
Chapter 94 - Apprenticeship	49
Chapter 95 - Department of Labor and Labor Regulations	49
Chapter 95 - Department of Labor and Labor Regulations (Continuation)	50
Chapter 96 - Employment Security	50
Chapter 97 - Workers' Compensation Act	50
Chapter 97 - Workers' Compensation Act (Continuation)	51

Chapter 98 - Burnt and Lost Records	51
Chapter 99 - Libel and Slander	51
Chapter 99A - Civil Remedies for Criminal Actions	51
Chapter 99B - Products Liability	51
Chapter 99C - Actions Relating to Winter Sports Safety and Accidents	51
Chapter 99D - Civil Rights	51
Chapter 99E - Special Liability Provisions	51
Chapter 100 - Monuments, Memorials and Parks	51
Chapter 101 - Names of Persons	51
Chapter 102 - Official Survey Base	51
Chapter 103 - Sundays, Holidays and Special Days	51
Chapter 104 - United States Lands	51
Chapter 104A - Degrees of Kinship	51
Chapter 104B - Hurricanes or Other Acts of Nature	51
Chapter 104C - Atomic Energy, Radioactivity and Ionizing Radiation [Repealed and Recodified.]	51
Chapter 104D - Southern States Energy Compact	51
Chapter 104E - North Carolina Radiation Protection Act	51
Chapter 104F - Southeast Interstate Low-Level Radioactive Waste Management Compact [Repealed]	51
Chapter 104G - North Carolina Low-Level Radioactive Waste Management Authority Act of 1987 [Repealed]	51
Chapter 105 - Taxation	51
Chapter 105 - Taxation (Continuation)	52
Chapter 105 - Taxation (Continuation)	53
Chapter 105 - Taxation (Continuation)	54
Chapter 105A - Setoff Debt Collection Act	55
Chapter 105B - Defaulted Student Loan Recovery Act	55
Chapter 106 - Agriculture	55
Chapter 106 - Agriculture (Continue)	56
Chapter 106 - Agriculture (Continue)	57
Chapter 107 - Agricultural Development Districts [Repealed.]	57
Chapter 108 - Social Services [Repealed and Recodified.]	57
Chapter 108A - Social Services	57
Chapter 108B - Community Action Programs	58
Chapter 108C Medicaid and Health Choice Provider Requirements.	58
Chapter 108D Medicaid Managed Care for Behavioral Health Services.	58
Chapter 109 - Bonds [Recodified.]	58
Chapter 110 - Child Welfare	58
Chapter 111 - Aid to the Blind	58
Chapter 112 - Confederate Homes and Pensions [Repealed.]	58
Chapter 113 - Conservation and Development	58
Chapter 113 - Conservation and Development (Continuation)	59

Chapter 113A - Pollution Control and Environment	59
Chapter 113A - Pollution Control and Environment (Continuation)	60
Chapter 113B - North Carolina Energy Policy Act of 1975	60
Chapter 114 - Department of Justice	60
Chapter 115 - Elementary and Secondary Education [Repealed.]	60
Chapter 115A - Community Colleges, Technical Institutes, and Industrial Education Centers [Repealed.]	60
Chapter 115B - Tuition and Fee Waivers	60
Chapter 115C - Elementary and Secondary Education	60
Chapter 115C - Elementary and Secondary Education (Continuation)	61
Chapter 115C - Elementary and Secondary Education (Continuation)	62
Chapter 115C - Elementary and Secondary Education (Continuation)	63
Chapter 115D - Community Colleges	63
Chapter 115E - Private Educational Facilities Finance Act [Recodified]	63
Chapter 116 - Higher Education	63
Chapter 116 - Higher Education (Continuation)	63
Chapter 116A - Escheats and Abandoned Property [Repealed.]	64
Chapter 116B - Escheats and Abandoned Property	64
Chapter 116C - Continuum of Education Programs	64
Chapter 116D - Higher Education Bonds	64
Chapter 117 - Electrification	64
Chapter 118 - Firemen's and Rescue Squad Workers' Relief and Pension Funds [Recodified.]	64
Chapter 118A - Firemen's Death Benefit Act [Repealed.]	64
Chapter 118B - Members of a Rescue Squad Death Benefit Act [Repealed.]	64
Chapter 119 - Gasoline and Oil Inspection and Regulation	64
Chapter 120 - General Assembly	65
Chapter 120 - General Assembly (Continuation)	66
Chapter 120 - General Assembly (Continuation)	67
Chapter 120C - Lobbying	67
Chapter 121 - Archives and History	67
Chapter 122 - Hospitals for the Mentally Disordered [Repealed.]	67
Chapter 122A - North Carolina Housing Finance Agency	67
Chapter 122B - North Carolina Agricultural Facilities Finance Act [Repealed.]	67
Chapter 122C - Mental Health, Developmental Disabilities, and Substance Abuse Act of 1985	67
Chapter 122C - Mental Health, Developmental Disabilities, and Substance Abuse Act of 1985 (Continuation)	68
Chapter 122D - North Carolina Agricultural Finance Act	68

Chapter 122E - North Carolina Housing Trust and Oil Overcharge Act	68
Chapter 123 - Impeachment	69
Chapter 123A - Industrial Development [Repealed.]	69
Chapter 124 - Internal Improvements	69
Chapter 125 - Libraries	69
Chapter 126 - State Personnel System	69
Chapter 127 - Militia [Repealed.]	69
Chapter 127A - Militia	69
Chapter 127B - Military Affairs	69
Chapter 127C - Advisory Commission on Military Affairs	69
Chapter 128 - Offices and Public Officers	69
Chapter 128 - Offices and Public Officers (Continuation)	70
Chapter 129 - Public Buildings and Grounds	70
Chapter 130 - Public Health [Repealed.]	70
Chapter 130A - Public Health	70
Chapter 130A - Public Health (Continuation)	71
Chapter 130A - Public Health (Continuation)	72
Chapter 130B - Hazardous Waste Management Commission [Repealed.]	72
Chapter 131 - Public Hospitals [Repealed.]	72
Chapter 131A - Health Care Facilities Finance Act	72
Chapter 131B - Licensing of Ambulatory Surgical Facilities [Repealed.]	72
Chapter 131C - Charitable Solicitation Licensure Act [Repealed.]	72
Chapter 131D - Inspection and Licensing of Facilities	72
Chapter 131E - Health Care Facilities and Services	72
Chapter 131E - Health Care Facilities and Services (Continuation)	73
Chapter 131F - Solicitation of Contributions	73
Chapter 132 - Public Records	73
Chapter 133 - Public Works	74
Chapter 134 - Youth Development [Recodified.]	74
Chapter 134A - Youth Services [Repealed.]	74
Chapter 135 - Retirement System for Teachers and State Employees; Social Security; Health Insurance Program for Children	74
Chapter 135 - Retirement System for Teachers and State Employees; Social Security; Health Insurance Program for Children	75
Chapter 136 - Transportation	75
Chapter 136 - Transportation (Continuation)	76
Chapter 137 - Rural Rehabilitation [Repealed.]	76
Chapter 138 - Salaries, Fees and Allowances	76
Chapter 138A - State Government Ethics Act	76
Chapter 139 - Soil and Water Conservation Districts	76

Chapter 140 - State Art Museum; Symphony and Art Societies	76
Chapter 140A - State Awards System	76
Chapter 141 - State Boundaries	76
Chapter 142 - State Debt	76
Chapter 143 - State Departments, Institutions, and Commissions	77
Chapter 143 - State Departments, Institutions, and Commissions (Continuation)	78
Chapter 143 - State Departments, Institutions, and Commissions (Continuation)	79
Chapter 143 - State Departments, Institutions, and Commissions (Continuation)	80
Chapter 143A - State Government Reorganization	80
Chapter 143B - Executive Organization Act of 1973	80
Chapter 143B - Executive Organization Act of 1973 (Continuation)	81
Chapter 143B - Executive Organization Act of 1973 (Continuation)	82
Chapter 143C - State Budget Act	83
Chapter 143D - The State Governmental Accountability and Internal Control Act	83
Chapter 144 - State Flag, Official Governmental Flags, Motto, and Colors	83
Chapter 145 - State Symbols and Other Official Adoptions.	83
Chapter 146 - State Lands	83
Chapter 147 - State Officers	83
Chapter 148 - State Prison System	84
Chapter 149 - State Song and Toast	84
Chapter 150 - Uniform Revocation of Licenses [Repealed.]	84
Chapter 150A - Administrative Procedure Act [Recodified.]	84
Chapter 150B - Administrative Procedure Act	84
Chapter 151 - Constables [Repealed.]	84
Chapter 152 - Coroners	84
Chapter 152A - County Medical Examiner [Repealed.]	84
Chapter 152A - County Medical Examiner [Repealed.] (Continuation)	85
Chapter 153 - Counties and County Commissioners [Repealed.]	85
Chapter 153A - Counties	85
Chapter 153B - Mountain Resources Planning Act	85
Chapter 153C - Uwharrie Regional Resources Act	85
Chapter 154 - County Surveyor [Repealed.]	85
Chapter 155 - County Treasurer [Repealed.]	85
Chapter 156 - Drainage	85
Chapter 156 – Drainage (Continuation)	86

Chapter 157 - Housing Authorities and Projects	86
Chapter 157A - Historic Properties Commissions [Transferred.]	86
Chapter 158 - Local Development	86
Chapter 159 - Local Government Finance	86
Chapter 159 - Local Government Finance (Continuation)	87
Chapter 159A - Pollution Abatement and Industrial Facilities Financing Act [Unconstitutional.]	87
Chapter 159B - Joint Municipal Electric Power and Energy Act	87
Chapter 159C - Industrial and Pollution Control Facilities Financing Act	87
Chapter 159D - The North Carolina Capital Facilities Financing Act	87
Chapter 159E - Registered Public Obligations Act	87
Chapter 159F - North Carolina Energy Development Authority [Repealed.]	87
Chapter 159G - Water Infrastructure	87
Chapter 159H - [Reserved.]	87
Chapter 159I - Solid Waste Management Loan Program and Local Government Special Obligation Bonds	87
Chapter 160 - Municipal Corporations [Repealed And Transferred.]	87
Chapter 160A - Cities and Towns	88
Chapter 160A - Cities and Towns (Continuation)	89
Chapter 160B - Consolidated City-County Act	89
Chapter 160C - Baseball Park Districts [Repealed.]	90
Chapter 161 - Register of Deeds	90
Chapter 162 - Sheriff	90
Chapter 162A - Water and Sewer Systems	90
Chapter 162B Continuity of Local Government in Emergency.	90
Chapter 163 Elections and Election Laws.	90
Chapter 163 Elections and Election Laws. (Continuation)	91
Chapter 164 Concerning the General Statutes of North Carolina.	92
Chapter 165 Veterans.	92
Chapter 166 Civil Preparedness Agencies [Repealed.]	92
Chapter 166A North Carolina Emergency Management Act.	92
Chapter 167 State Civil Air Patrol [Repealed.]	92
Chapter 168 Persons with Disabilities.	92
Chapter 168A Persons With Disabilities Protection Act.	92

§ 20-289. License fees.

(a)	The license fee for each fiscal year, or part thereof, shall be as follows:

(1)	For motor vehicle dealers, distributors, distributor branches, and wholesalers, seventy dollars ($70.00) for each place of business.

(2)	For manufacturers, one hundred fifty dollars ($150.00) and for each factory branch in this State, one hundred dollars ($100.00).

(3)	For motor vehicle sales representatives, fifteen dollars ($15.00).

(4)	For factory representatives, or distributor representatives, fifteen dollars ($15.00).

(5)	Repealed by Session Laws 1991, c. 662, s. 4.

(b)	The fees collected under this section shall be credited to the Highway Fund. These fees are in addition to all other taxes and fees. (1955, c. 1243, s. 5; 1969, c. 593; 1977, c. 802, s. 8; 1981, c. 690, s. 16; 1991, c. 662, s. 4; c. 689, s. 335; 2005-276, s. 44.1(o).)

§ 20-290. Licenses to specify places of business; display of license and list of salesmen; advertising.

(a)	The license of a motor vehicle dealer shall list each of the dealer's established salesrooms in this State. A license of a manufacturer, factory branch, distributor, distributor branch, or wholesaler shall list each of the license holder's places of business in this State. A license shall be conspicuously displayed at each place of business. In the event the location of a business changes, the Division shall endorse the change of location on the license, without charge.

(b)	Each dealer shall keep a current list of his licensed salesmen, showing the name of each licensed salesman, posted in a conspicuous place in each place of business.

(c) Whenever any licensee places an advertisement in any newspaper or publication, the licensee's name shall appear in the advertisement. (1955, c. 1243, s. 6; 1975, c. 716, s. 5; 1991, c. 662, s. 5; 2005-99, s. 3.)

§ 20-291. Representatives to carry license and display it on request; license to name employer.

Every person to whom a sales representative, factory representative, or distributor representative license is issued shall carry the license when engaged in business, and shall display it upon request. The license shall state the name of the representative's employer. If the representative changes employers, the representative shall immediately apply to the Division for a license that states the name of the representative's new employer. The fee for issuing a license stating the name of a new employer is ten dollars ($10.00). (1955, c. 1243, s. 7; 1975, c. 716, s. 5; 1991, c. 662, s. 6; c. 689, s. 336; 2005-99, s. 4; 2005-276, s. 44.1(r).)

§ 20-292. Dealers may display motor vehicles for sale at retail only at established salesrooms.

A new or used motor vehicle dealer may display a motor vehicle for sale at retail only at the dealer's established salesroom, unless the display is of a motor vehicle that meets any of the following descriptions:

(1) Contains the dealer's name or other sales information and is used by the dealer as a "demonstrator" for transportation purposes.

(2) Is displayed at a trade show or exhibit at which no selling activities relating to the vehicle take place.

(3) Is displayed at the home or place of business of a customer at the request of the customer.

This section does not apply to recreational vehicles, house trailers, or boat, animal, camping, or other utility trailers. (1955, c. 1243, s. 8; 1991, c. 662, s. 7.)

§ 20-292.1. Supplemental temporary license for sale of antique and specialty vehicles.

Any dealer licensed as a motor vehicle dealer under this Article may apply to the Commissioner and receive, at no additional charge, a supplemental temporary license authorizing the off-premises sales of antique motor vehicles and specialty motor vehicles for a period not to exceed 10 consecutive calendar days. To obtain a temporary supplemental license for the off-premises sale of antique motor vehicles and specialty motor vehicles, the applicant shall:

(1)   Be licensed as a motor vehicle dealer under this Article.

(2)   Notify the applicable local office of the Division of the specific dates and location for which the license is requested.

(3)   Display a sign at the licensed location clearly identifying the dealer.

(4)   Keep and maintain the records required for the sale of motor vehicles under this Article.

(5)   Provide staff to work at the temporary location for the duration of the off-premises sale.

(6)   Meet any local government permitting requirements.

(7)   Have written permission from the property owner to sell at the location.

For purposes of this section, the term "antique motor vehicle" shall mean any motor vehicle for private use manufactured at least 25 years prior to the current model year, and the term "specialty motor vehicle" shall mean any model or series of motor vehicle for private use manufactured at least three years prior to the current model year of which no more than 5,000 vehicles were sold within the United States during the model year the vehicle was manufactured.

This section does not apply to a nonselling motor vehicle show or public display of new motor vehicles. (2003-113, s. 1.)

§ 20-293: Repealed by Session Laws 1993, c. 440, s. 10.

§ 20-294. Grounds for denying, suspending or revoking licenses.

The Division may deny, suspend, or revoke a license issued under this Article for any one or more of the following grounds:

(1)   Making a material misstatement in an application for a license.

(2)   Willfully and intentionally failing to comply with this Article, Article 15 of this Chapter, or G.S. 20-52.1, 20-75, 20-79.1, 20-79.2, 20-108, 20-109, or a rule adopted by the Division under this Article.

(3)   Failing to have an established salesroom, if the license holder is a motor vehicle dealer, or failing to have an established office, if the license holder is a wholesaler.

(4)   Willfully defrauding any retail buyer, to the buyer's damage, or any other person in the conduct of the licensee's business.

(5)   Employing fraudulent devices, methods or practices in connection with compliance with the requirements under the laws of this State with respect to the retaking of motor vehicles under retail installment contracts and the redemption and resale of such motor vehicles.

(6)   Using unfair methods of competition or unfair deceptive acts or practices.

(7)   Knowingly advertising by any means, any assertion, representation or statement of fact which is untrue, misleading or deceptive in any particular relating to the conduct of the business licensed or for which a license is sought.

(8)   Knowingly advertising a used motor vehicle for sale as a new motor vehicle.

(9)   Being convicted of an offense set forth under G.S. 20-106, 20-106.1, 20-107, or 20-112 while holding such a license or within five years next preceding the date of filing the application; or being convicted of a felony involving moral turpitude under the laws of this State, another state, or the United States.

(10) Submitting a bad check to the Division of Motor Vehicles in payment of highway use taxes collected by the licensee.

(11) Knowingly giving an incorrect certificate of title, or failing to give a certificate of title to a purchaser, a lienholder, or the Division, as appropriate, after a vehicle is sold.

(12) Making a material misstatement in an application for a dealer license plate.

(13) Failure to pay a civil penalty imposed under G.S. 20-287. (1955, c. 1243, s. 10; 1963, c. 1102; 1967, c. 1126, s. 2; 1975, c. 716, s. 5; 1977, c. 560, s. 3; 1983, c. 704, s. 4; 1985, c. 687; ss. 1, 2; 1991, c. 193, s. 2; 1993, c. 440, s. 11; 2001-345, ss. 3, 4; 2010-132, s. 16.)

§ 20-295. Action on application.

The Division shall either grant or deny an application for a license within 30 days after receiving it. Any applicant denied a license shall, upon filing a written request within 30 days, be given a hearing at the time and place determined by the Commissioner or a person designated by the Commissioner. A hearing shall be public and shall be held with reasonable promptness. (1955, c. 1243, s. 11; 1975, c. 716, s. 5; 1993, c. 440, s. 1.)

§ 20-296. Notice and hearing upon denial, suspension, revocation or refusal to renew license.

No license shall be suspended or revoked or denied, or renewal thereof refused, until a written notice of the complaint made has been furnished to the licensee against whom the same is directed, and a hearing thereon has been had before the Commissioner, or a person designated by him. At least 10 days' written notice of the time and place of such hearing shall be given to the licensee by certified mail with return receipt requested to his last known address as shown on his license or other record of information in possession of the Division. At any such hearing, the licensee shall have the right to be heard personally or by counsel. After hearing, the Division shall have power to suspend, revoke or refuse to renew the license in question. Immediate notice of any such action shall be given to the licensee in the manner herein provided in the case of notices of hearing. (1955, c. 1243, s. 12; 1975, c. 716, s. 5; 1981, c. 108.)

§ 20-297. Retention and inspection of certain records.

(a)   Vehicles. - A dealer must keep a record of all vehicles received by the dealer and all vehicles sold by the dealer. The records must contain the information that the Division requires. A dealer may keep and maintain records at the dealership facility where the vehicles were sold or at another established office located within this State provided that the location and the name of a designated contact agent are provided to the Division and the records can be made available for inspection by the Division within a reasonable period of time after being requested by the Division.

(b)   Inspection. - The Division may inspect the pertinent books, records, letters, and contracts of a licensee relating to any written complaint made to the Division against the licensee. (1955, c. 1243, s. 13; 1975, c. 716, s. 5; 1995, c. 163, s. 5; 2007-481, s. 3.)

§ 20-297.1. Franchise-related form agreements.

(a)   All franchise-related form agreements, as defined in this subsection, offered to a motor vehicle dealer in this State shall provide that all terms and conditions in the agreement inconsistent with any of the laws or rules of this State are of no force and effect. For purposes of this section, the term "franchise-related form agreements" means one or more contracts between a franchised motor vehicle dealer and a manufacturer, factory branch, distributor, or distributor branch, including a written communication from a manufacturer or distributor in which a duty is imposed on the franchised motor vehicle dealer under which:

(1)   The franchised motor vehicle dealer is granted the right to sell and service new motor vehicles manufactured or distributed by the manufacturer or distributor or only to service motor vehicles under the contract and a manufacturer's warranty;

(2) The franchised motor vehicle dealer is a component of the manufacturer or distributor's distribution system as an independent business;

(3) The franchised motor vehicle dealer is substantially associated with the manufacturer or distributor's trademark, trade name, and commercial symbol;

(4) The franchised motor vehicle dealer's business substantially relies on the manufacturer or distributor for a continued supply of motor vehicles, parts, and accessories; or

(5) Any right, duty, or obligation granted or imposed by this Chapter is affected.

(b) Notwithstanding the terms of any franchise or agreement, it shall be unlawful for any manufacturer, factory branch, distributor, or distributor branch to offer to a dealer, revise, modify, or replace a franchise-related form agreement, as defined above in this section, which agreement, modification, or replacement may adversely affect or alter the rights, obligations, or liability of a motor vehicle dealer or may adversely impair the sales, service obligations, investment, or profitability of any motor vehicle dealer located in this State, unless:

(1) The manufacturer, factory branch, distributor, or distributor branch provides prior written notice by registered or certified mail to each affected dealer, the Commissioner, and the North Carolina Automobile Dealers Association, Inc., of the modification or replacement in the form and within the time frame set forth within this section and in subsection (c) of this section; and

(2) If a protest is filed under this section, the Commissioner approves the modification or replacement.

(c) The notice required by subdivision (b)(1) of this section shall:

(1) Be given not later than the 60th day before the effective date of the modification or replacement;

(2) Contain on its first page a conspicuous statement that reads: "NOTICE TO DEALER: YOU MAY BE ENTITLED TO FILE A PROTEST WITH THE COMMISSIONER OF THE NORTH CAROLINA DIVISION OF MOTOR VEHICLES AND HAVE A HEARING IN WHICH YOU MAY PROTEST THE PROPOSED INITIAL OFFERING, MODIFICATION, OR REPLACEMENT OF

CERTAIN FRANCHISE-RELATED FORM AGREEMENTS UNDER THE TERMS OF THE MOTOR VEHICLE DEALERS AND MANUFACTURERS LICENSING LAW, IF YOU OPPOSE THIS ACTION"; and

(3)   Contain a separate letter or statement that identifies all substantive modifications or revisions and the principal reasons for each such modification or revision.

(d)   A franchised dealer may file a protest with the Commissioner of the offering, modification, or replacement pursuant to this section not later than the latter of:

(1)   The 60th day after the date of the receipt of the notice; or

(2)   The time specified in the notice.

(e)   After a protest is filed, the Commissioner shall determine whether the manufacturer, factory branch, distributor, or distributor branch has established by a preponderance of the evidence that there is good cause for the proposed offering, modification, or replacement. The prior franchise-related form agreement, if any, continues in effect until the Commissioner resolves the protest.

(f)   The Commissioner is authorized and directed to investigate and prevent violations of this section, including inconsistencies of any franchise-related form agreement with the provisions of this Article.

(g)   Nothing contained in this section shall in any way limit a dealer's rights under any other provision of this Article or other applicable law. (1997-319, s. 1; 2005-409, s. 1.)

§ 20-298. Insurance.

It shall be unlawful for any dealer or salesman or any employee of any dealer, to coerce or offer anything of value to any purchaser of a motor vehicle to provide any type of insurance coverage on said motor vehicle. No dealer, salesman or representative of either shall accept any policy as collateral on any vehicle sold by him to secure an interest in such vehicle in any company not qualified under the insurance laws of this State: Provided, nothing in this Article shall prevent a dealer or his representative from requiring adequate insurance coverage on a motor vehicle which is the subject of an installment sale. (1955, c. 1243, s. 14.)

§ 20-299. Acts of officers, directors, partners, salesmen and other representatives.

(a)   If a licensee is a copartnership or a corporation, it shall be sufficient cause for the denial, suspension or revocation of a license that any officer, director or partner of the copartnership or corporation has committed any act or omitted any duty which would be cause for refusing, suspending or revoking a license to such party as an individual. Each licensee shall be responsible for the acts of any or all of his salesmen while acting as his agent.

(b)   Every licensee who is a manufacturer or a factory branch shall be responsible for the acts of any or all of its agents and representatives while acting in the conduct of said licensee's business whether or not such licensee approved, authorized, or had knowledge of such acts. (1955, c. 1243, s. 15; 1973, c. 559.)

§ 20-300. Appeals from actions of Commissioner.

Appeals from actions of the Commissioner shall be governed by the provisions of Chapter 150B of the General Statutes. (1955, c. 1243, s. 16; 1973, c. 1331, s. 3; 1987, c. 827, s. 1.)

§ 20-301. Powers of Commissioner.

(a)   The Commissioner shall promote the interests of the retail buyer of motor vehicles.

(b)   The Commissioner shall have power to prevent unfair methods of competition and unfair or deceptive acts or practices and other violations of this Article. Any franchised new motor vehicle dealer who believes that a manufacturer, factory branch, distributor, or distributor branch with whom the dealer holds a currently valid franchise has violated or is currently violating any provision of this Article may file a petition before the Commissioner setting forth the factual and legal basis for such violations. The Commissioner shall promptly forward a copy of the petition to the named manufacturer, factory branch, distributor, or distributor branch requesting a reply to the petition within 30 days. Allowing for sufficient time for the parties to conduct discovery, the Commissioner or his designee shall then hold an evidentiary hearing and render findings of fact and conclusions of law based on the evidence presented. Any parties to a hearing by the Commissioner concerning the establishment or relocating of a new motor vehicle dealer shall have a right of review of the decision in a court of competent jurisdiction pursuant to Chapter 150B of the General Statutes.

(c)   The Commissioner shall have the power in hearings arising under this Article to enter scheduling orders and limit the time and scope of discovery; to determine the date, time, and place where hearings are to be held; to subpoena witnesses; to take depositions of witnesses; and to administer oaths.

(d)   The Commissioner may, whenever he shall believe from evidence submitted to him that any person has been or is violating any provision of this Article, in addition to any other remedy, bring an action in the name of the State against that person and any other persons concerned or in any way participating in, or about to participate in practices or acts so in violation, to enjoin any persons from continuing the violations.

(e)   The Commissioner may issue rules and regulations to implement the provisions of this section and to establish procedures related to administrative proceedings commenced under this section.

(f)   In the event that a dealer, who is permitted or required to file a notice, protest, or petition before the Commissioner within a certain period of time in order to adjudicate, enforce, or protect rights afforded the dealer under this Article, voluntarily elects to appeal a policy, determination, or decision of the manufacturer through an appeals board or internal grievance procedure of the manufacturer, or to participate in or refer the matter to mediation, arbitration, or other alternative dispute resolution procedure or process established or endorsed by the manufacturer, the applicable period of time for the dealer to file the notice, protest, or petition before the Commissioner under this Article shall not commence until the manufacturer's appeal board or internal grievance procedure, mediation, arbitration, or appeals process of the manufacturer has been completed and the dealer has received notice in writing of the final decision or result of the procedure or process. Nothing, however, contained in this subsection shall be deemed to require that any dealer exhaust any internal grievance or other alternative dispute process required or established by the manufacturer before seeking redress from the Commissioner as provided in this Article.

(g) Notwithstanding any other statute, regulation, or rule or the existence of a pending legal or administrative proceeding in any other forum any franchised new motor vehicle dealer or any manufacturer, factory branch, distributor, or distributor branch may elect to file a petition before the Commissioner for resolution of any dispute that may arise with respect to any of the rights or obligations of the dealer or of the manufacturer, factory branch, distributor, or distributor branch related to a franchise or franchise-related form agreement. The Commissioner shall have the authority to apply principles of law, equity, and good faith in determining such matters. The filing of a petition by a dealer or a manufacturer, factory branch, distributor, or distributor branch pursuant to this section shall not preclude the party filing the petition from pursuing any other form of recourse it may have, either before the Commissioner or in another form, including any damages and injunctive relief. The Commissioner shall have the authority to receive and evaluate the facts in the matter of controversy and render a decision by entering an order which shall thereafter become binding and enforceable with respect to the parties, subject to the right of review of the decision in a court of competent jurisdiction pursuant to Chapter 150B of the General Statutes. (1955, c. 1243, s. 17; 1983, c. 704, s. 23; 1991, c. 510, s. 1; 1997-319, s. 2; 1999-335, s. 1; 2011-290, s. 3.)

§ 20-301.1. Notice of additional charges against dealer's account; informal appeals procedure.

(a) Notwithstanding the terms of any contract, franchise, novation, or agreement, it shall be unlawful for any manufacturer, factory branch, distributor, or distributor branch to charge or assess one of its franchised motor vehicle dealers located in this State, or to charge or debit the account of the franchised motor vehicle dealer for merchandise, tools, or equipment, or other charges or amounts which total more [than] five thousand dollars ($5,000), other than the published cost of new motor vehicles, and merchandise, tools, or equipment specifically ordered by the franchised motor vehicle dealer, unless the franchised motor vehicle dealer receives a detailed itemized description of the nature and amount of each charge in writing at least 10 days prior to the date the charge or account debit is to become effective or due. For purposes of this subsection, the prior written notice required pursuant to this subsection includes, but is not limited to, all charges or debits to a dealer's account for advertising or advertising materials; advertising or showroom displays; customer informational materials; computer or communications hardware or software; special tools; equipment; dealership operation guides; Internet programs; and any additional charges or surcharges made or proposed for merchandise, tools, or equipment previously charged to the dealer; and any other charges or amounts which total more than five thousand dollars ($5,000). If the franchised new motor vehicle dealer disputes all or any portion of an actual or proposed charge or debit to the dealer's account, the dealer may proceed as provided in G.S. 20-301(b) and G.S. 20-308.1. Upon the filing of a petition pursuant to G.S. 20-301(b) or a civil action pursuant to G.S. 20-308.1, the affected manufacturer, factory branch, distributor, or distributor branch shall not require payment from the dealer, or debit or charge the dealer's account, unless and until a final judgment supporting the payment or charge has been rendered by the Commissioner or court.

(b)   Any franchised new motor vehicle dealer who seeks to challenge an actual or proposed charge, debit, payment, reimbursement, or credit to the franchised new motor vehicle dealer or to the franchised new motor vehicle dealer's account in an amount less than or equal to ten thousand dollars ($10,000) and that is in violation of this Article or contrary to the terms of the franchise may, prior to filing a formal petition before the Commissioner as provided in G.S. 20-301(b) or a civil action in any court of competent jurisdiction under G.S. 20-308.1, request and obtain a mediated settlement conference as provided in this subsection. Unless objection to the timeliness of the franchised new motor vehicle dealer's request for mediation under this subsection is waived in writing by the affected manufacturer, factory branch, distributor, or distributor branch, a franchised new motor vehicle dealer's request to mediate must be sent to the Commissioner within 75 days after the franchised new motor vehicle dealer's receipt of written notice from a manufacturer, factory branch, distributor, or distributor branch of the charges, debits, payments, reimbursements, or credits challenged by the franchised new motor vehicle dealer. If the franchised new motor vehicle dealer has requested in writing that the manufacturer, factory branch, distributor, or distributor branch review the questioned charges, debits, payments, reimbursements, or credits, a franchised new motor vehicle dealer's request to mediate must be sent to the Commissioner within 30 days after the franchised new motor vehicle dealer's receipt of the final written determination on the issue from the manufacturer, factory branch, distributor, or distributor branch.

(1) It is the policy and purpose of this subsection to implement a system of settlement events that are designed to reduce the cost of litigation under this Article to the general public and the parties, to focus the parties' attention on settlement rather than on trial preparation, and to provide a structured opportunity for settlement negotiations to take place.

(2) The franchised new motor vehicle dealer shall send a letter to the Commissioner by certified or registered mail, return receipt requested, identifying the actual or proposed charges the franchised new motor vehicle dealer seeks to challenge and the reason or basis for the challenge. The charges, debits, payments, reimbursements, or credits challenged by the franchised new motor vehicle dealer need not be related, and multiple issues may be resolved in a single proceeding. The franchised new motor vehicle dealer shall send a copy of the letter to the affected manufacturer, factory branch, distributor, or distributor branch, addressed to the current district, zone, or regional manager in charge of overseeing the dealer's operations, or the registered agent for acceptance of legal process in this State. Upon the mailing of a letter to the Commissioner and the manufacturer, factory branch, distributor, or distributor branch pursuant to this subsection, any chargeback to or any payment required of a franchised new motor vehicle dealer by a manufacturer, factory branch, distributor, or distributor branch shall be stayed during the pendency of the mediation. Upon the mailing of a letter to the Commissioner and manufacturer, factory branch, distributor, or distributor branch pursuant to this subsection, any statute of limitation or other time limitation for filing a petition before the Commissioner or civil action shall be tolled during the pendency of the mediation.

(3) Upon receipt of the written request of the franchised new motor vehicle dealer, the Commissioner shall appoint a mediator and send notice of that appointment to the parties. A person is qualified to serve as mediator as provided by this subdivision if the person is certified to serve as a mediator under Rule 8 of the North Carolina Rules Implementing Statewide Mediated Settlement Conferences in Superior Court Civil Actions and does not represent motor vehicle dealers or manufacturers, factory branches, distributors, or distributor branches. A mediator acting pursuant to this subdivision shall have judicial immunity in the same manner and to the same extent as a judge of the General Court of Justice.

(4) The parties shall by written agreement select a venue and schedule for the mediated settlement conference conducted under this subsection. If the parties are unable to agree on a venue and schedule, the mediator shall select

a venue and schedule. Except by written agreement of all parties, a mediation proceeding and mediated settlement conference under this subsection shall be held in North Carolina.

(5)   In this subsection, "mediation" means a nonbinding forum in which an impartial person, the mediator, facilitates communication between parties to promote reconciliation, settlement, or understanding among them. A mediator may not impose his or her own judgment on the issues for that of the parties.

(6)   At least 10 days prior to the mediated settlement conference, the affected manufacturer, factory branch, distributor, or distributor branch shall, by certified or registered mail, return receipt requested, send the mediator and the franchised new motor vehicle dealer a detailed response to the allegations raised in the franchised new motor vehicle dealer's written request. The mediation may be conducted by officers or employees of the parties themselves without the appearance of legal counsel. However, at least 10 days prior to the mediated settlement conference, either party may give notice to the other and to the mediator of its intention to appear at the mediation with legal counsel, in which event either party may appear at the mediation with legal counsel.

(7)   A mediation proceeding conducted pursuant to this subsection shall be complete not later than the sixtieth day after the date of the Commissioner's notice of the appointment of the mediator; this deadline may be extended by written agreement of the parties. The parties shall be solely responsible for the compensation and expenses of the mediator on a 50/50 basis. The Commissioner is not liable for the compensation paid or to be paid a mediator employed pursuant to this subsection.

(8)   A party may attend a mediated settlement conference telephonically in lieu of personal appearance. If a party or other person required to attend a mediated settlement conference fails to attend without good cause, the Commissioner may impose upon the party or person any appropriate monetary sanction, including the payment of fines, attorneys' fees, mediator fees, expenses, and loss of earnings incurred by persons attending the conference.

(9)   If the mediation fails to result in a resolution of the dispute, the franchised new motor vehicle dealer may proceed as provided in G.S. 20-301(b) and G.S. 20-308.1. Upon the filing of a petition pursuant to G.S. 20-301(b) or a civil action pursuant to G.S. 20-308.1, the affected manufacturer, factory branch, distributor, or distributor branch shall not require payment from the dealer, or debit or charge the dealer's account, unless and until a final judgment

supporting the payment or charge has been rendered by the Commissioner or court. All communications made during a mediation proceeding, including, but not limited to, those communications made during a mediated settlement conference are presumed to be made in compromise negotiation and shall be governed by Rule 408 of the North Carolina Rules of Evidence. (2001-510, s. 1; 2011-290, s. 4.)

§ 20-302. Rules and regulations.

The Commissioner may make such rules and regulations, not inconsistent with the provisions of this Article, as he shall deem necessary or proper for the effective administration and enforcement of this Article, provided that a copy of such rules and regulations shall be mailed to each motor vehicle dealer licensee 30 days prior to the effective date of such rules and regulations. (1955, c. 1243, s. 18.)

§ 20-303. Installment sales to be evidenced by written instrument; statement to be delivered to buyer.

(a) Every retail installment sale shall be evidenced by one or more instruments in writing, which shall contain all the agreements of the parties and shall be signed by the buyer.

(b) For every retail installment sale, prior to or about the time of the delivery of the motor vehicle, the seller shall deliver to the buyer a written statement describing clearly the motor vehicle sold to the buyer, the cash sale price thereof, the cash paid down by the buyer, the amount credited the buyer for any trade-in and a description of the motor vehicle traded, the amount of the finance charge, the amount of any other charge specifying its purpose, the net balance due from the buyer, the terms of the payment of such net balance and a summary of any insurance protection to be effected. The written statement shall be signed by the buyer. (1955, c. 1243, s. 19; 2007-513, s. 1.)

§ 20-304. Coercion of retail dealer by manufacturer or distributor in connection with installment sales contract prohibited.

(a) It shall be unlawful for any manufacturer, wholesaler or distributor, or any officer, agent or representative of either, to coerce, or attempt to coerce, any retail motor vehicle dealer or prospective retail motor vehicle dealer in this State to sell, assign or transfer any retail installment sales contract, obtained by such dealer in connection with the sale by him in this State of motor vehicles manufactured or sold by such manufacturer, wholesaler, or distributor, to a specified finance company or class of such companies, or to any other specified persons, by any of the acts or means hereinafter set forth, namely:

(1) By any statement, suggestion, promise or threat that such manufacturer, wholesaler, or distributor will in any manner benefit or injure such dealer, whether such statement, suggestion, threat or promise is expressed or implied, or made directly or indirectly,

(2) By any act that will benefit or injure such dealer,

(3) By any contract, or any expressed or implied offer of contract, made directly or indirectly to such dealer, for handling motor vehicles, on the condition that such dealer sell, assign or transfer his retail installment sales contract thereon, in this State, to a specified finance company or class of such companies, or to any other specified person,

(4) By any expressed or implied statement or representation, made directly or indirectly, that such dealer is under any obligation whatsoever to sell, assign or transfer any of his retail sales contracts, in this State, on motor vehicles manufactured or sold by such manufacturer, wholesaler, or distributor to such finance company, or class of companies, or other specified person, because of any relationship or affiliation between such manufacturer, wholesaler, or distributor and such finance company or companies or such other specified person or persons.

(b) Any such statements, threats, promises, acts, contracts, or offers of contracts, when the effect thereof may be to lessen or eliminate competition, or tend to create a monopoly, are declared unfair trade practices and unfair methods of competition and against the public policy of this State, are unlawful and are hereby prohibited. (1955, c. 1243, s. 20.)

§ 20-305. Coercing dealer to accept commodities not ordered; threatening to cancel franchise; preventing transfer of ownership; granting additional franchises; terminating franchises without good cause; preventing family succession.

It shall be unlawful for any manufacturer, factory branch, distributor, or distributor branch, or any field representative, officer, agent, or any representative whatsoever of any of them:

(1)   To require, coerce, or attempt to coerce any dealer to accept delivery of any motor vehicle or vehicles, parts or accessories therefor, or any other commodities, which shall not have been ordered by that dealer, or to accept delivery of any motor vehicle or vehicles which have been equipped in a manner other than as specified by the dealer.

(2)   To require, coerce, or attempt to coerce any dealer to enter into any agreement with such manufacturer, factory branch, distributor, or distributor branch, or representative thereof, or do any other act unfair to such dealer, by threatening to cancel any franchise existing between such manufacturer, factory branch, distributor, distributor branch, or representative thereof, and such dealer;

(3)   (See Editor's note for applicability) Unfairly without due regard to the equities of the dealer, and without just provocation, to cancel the franchise of such dealer;

(4)   Notwithstanding the terms of any franchise agreement, to prevent or refuse to approve the sale or transfer of the ownership of a dealership by the sale of the business, stock transfer, or otherwise, or the transfer, sale or assignment of a dealer franchise, or a change in the executive management or principal operator of the dealership, change in use of an existing facility to provide for the sales or service of one or more additional line-makes of new motor vehicles, or relocation of the dealership to another site within the dealership's relevant market area, if the Commissioner has determined, if requested in writing by the dealer within 30 days after receipt of an objection to the proposed transfer, sale, assignment, relocation, or change, and after a hearing on the matter, that the failure to permit or honor the transfer, sale, assignment, relocation, or change is unreasonable under the circumstances. No franchise may be transferred, sold, assigned, relocated, or the executive management or principal operators changed, or the use of an existing facility changed, unless the franchisor has been given at least 30 days' prior written

notice as to the proposed transferee's name and address, financial ability, and qualifications of the proposed transferee, a copy of the purchase agreement between the dealership and the proposed transferee, the identity and qualifications of the persons proposed to be involved in executive management or as principal operators, and the location and site plans of any proposed relocation or change in use of a dealership facility. The franchisor shall send the dealership and the proposed transferee notice of objection, by registered or certified mail, return receipt requested, to the proposed transfer, sale, assignment, relocation, or change within 30 days after receipt of notice from the dealer, as provided in this section. The notice of objection shall state in detail all factual and legal bases for the objection on the part of the franchisor to the proposed transfer, sale, assignment, relocation, or change that is specifically referenced in this subdivision. An objection to a proposed transfer, sale, assignment, relocation, or change in the executive management or principal operator of the dealership or change in the use of the facility may only be premised upon the factual and legal bases specifically referenced in this subdivision or G.S. 20-305(11), as it relates to change in the use of a facility. A manufacturer's notice of objection which is based upon factual or legal issues that are not specifically referenced in this subdivision or G.S. 20-305(11) with respect to a change in the use of an existing facility as being issues upon which the Commissioner shall base his determination shall not be effective to preserve the franchisor's right to object to the proposed transfer sale, assignment, relocation, or change, provided the dealership or proposed transferee has submitted written notice, as required above, as to the proposed transferee's name and address, financial ability, and qualifications of the proposed transferee, a copy of the purchase agreement between the dealership and the proposed transferee, the identity and qualifications of the persons proposed to be involved in the executive management or as principal operators, and the location and site plans of any proposed relocation or change in the use of an existing facility. Failure by the franchisor to send notice of objection within 30 days shall constitute waiver by the franchisor of any right to object to the proposed transfer, sale, assignment, relocation, or change. If the franchisor requires additional information to complete its review, the franchisor shall notify the dealership within 15 days after receipt of the proposed transferee's name and address, financial ability, and qualifications, a copy of the purchase agreement between the dealership and the proposed transferee, the identity and qualifications of the persons proposed to be involved in executive management or as principal operators, and the location and site plans of any proposed relocation or change in use of the dealership facility. If the franchisor fails to request additional information from the dealer or proposed transferee within 15 days of receipt of this initial information, the 30-day time period within which the franchisor may provide notice of objection shall be deemed to run from the initial receipt date. Otherwise, the 30-day time period within which the franchisor may provide notice of objection shall run from the date the franchisor has received the supplemental information requested from the dealer or proposed transferee; provided, however, that failure by the franchisor to send notice of objection within 60 days of the franchisor's receipt of the initial information from the dealer shall constitute waiver by the franchisor of any right to object to the proposed transfer, sale, assignment, relocation, or change. With respect to a proposed transfer of ownership, sale, or assignment, the sole issue for determination by the Commissioner and the sole issue upon which the Commissioner shall hear or consider evidence is whether, by reason of lack of good moral character, lack of general business experience, or lack of financial ability, the proposed transferee is unfit to own the dealership. For purposes of this subdivision, the refusal by the manufacturer to accept a proposed transferee who is of good moral character and who otherwise meets the written, reasonable, and uniformly applied business experience and financial requirements, if any, required by the manufacturer of owners of its franchised automobile dealerships is presumed to demonstrate the manufacturer's failure to prove that the proposed transferee is unfit to own the dealership. With respect to a proposed change in the executive management or principal operator of the dealership, the sole issue for determination by the Commissioner and the sole issue on which the Commissioner shall hear or consider evidence shall be whether, by reason of lack of training, lack of prior experience, poor past performance, or poor character, the proposed candidate for a position within the executive management or as principal operator of the dealership is unfit for the position. For purposes of this subdivision, the refusal by the manufacturer to accept a proposed candidate for executive management or as principal operator who is of good moral character and who otherwise meets the written, reasonable, and uniformly applied standards or qualifications, if any, of the manufacturer relating to the business experience and prior performance of executive management required by the manufacturers of its dealers is presumed to demonstrate the manufacturer's failure to prove the proposed candidate for executive management or as principal operator is unfit to serve the capacity. With respect to a proposed change in use of a dealership facility to provide for the sales or service of one or more additional line-makes of new motor vehicles, the sole issue for determination by the Commissioner is whether the new motor vehicle dealer has a reasonable line of credit for each make or line of motor vehicle and remains in compliance with any reasonable capital standards and facilities requirements of the manufacturer or distributor. The reasonable facilities requirements of the manufacturer or distributor shall not include any requirement that a new motor vehicle dealer establish or maintain exclusive facilities, personnel, or display space. With respect to a proposed relocation or other proposed change, the issue for determination by the Commissioner is whether the proposed relocation or other change is unreasonable under the circumstances. For purposes of this subdivision, the refusal by the manufacturer to agree to a proposed relocation which meets the written, reasonable, and uniformly applied standards or criteria, if any, of the manufacturer relating to dealer relocations is presumed to demonstrate that the manufacturer's failure to prove the proposed relocation is unreasonable under the circumstances. The manufacturer shall have the burden of proof before the Commissioner under this subdivision. It is unlawful for a manufacturer to, in any way, condition its approval of a proposed transfer, sale, assignment, change in the dealer's executive management, principal operator, or appointment of a designated successor, on the existing or proposed dealer's willingness to construct a new facility, renovate the existing facility, acquire or refrain from acquiring one or more line-makes of vehicles, separate or divest one or more line-makes of vehicle, or establish or maintain exclusive facilities, personnel, or display space. It is unlawful for a manufacturer to, in any way, condition its approval of a proposed relocation on the existing or proposed dealer's willingness to acquire or refrain from acquiring one or more line-makes of vehicles, separate or divest one or more line-makes of vehicle, or establish or maintain exclusive facilities, personnel, or display space. The opinion or determination of a franchisor that the continued existence of one of its franchised dealers situated in this State is not viable, or that the dealer holds or fails to hold licensing rights for the sale of other line-makes of vehicles in a manner consistent with the franchisor's existing or future distribution or marketing plans, shall not constitute a lawful basis for the franchisor to fail or refuse to approve a dealer's proposed change in use of a dealership facility or relocation: provided, however, that nothing contained in this subdivision shall be deemed to prevent or prohibit a franchisor from failing to approve a dealer's proposed relocation on grounds that the specific site or facility proposed by the dealer is otherwise unreasonable under the circumstances. Approval of a relocation pursuant to this subdivision shall not in itself constitute the franchisor's representation or assurance of the dealer's viability at that location.

(5) To enter into a franchise establishing an additional new motor vehicle dealer or relocating an existing new motor vehicle dealer into a relevant market area where the same line make is then represented without first notifying in writing the Commissioner and each new motor vehicle dealer in that line make in the relevant market area of the intention to establish an additional dealer or to relocate an existing dealer within or into that market area. Within 30 days of receiving such notice or within 30 days after the end of any appeal procedure

provided by the manufacturer, any new motor vehicle dealer may file with the Commissioner a protest to the establishing or relocating of the new motor vehicle dealer. When a protest is filed, the Commissioner shall promptly inform the manufacturer that a timely protest has been filed, and that the manufacturer shall not establish or relocate the proposed new motor vehicle dealer until the Commissioner has held a hearing and has determined that there is good cause for permitting the addition or relocation of such new motor vehicle dealer.

a. This section does not apply:

1. To the relocation of an existing new motor vehicle dealer within that dealer's relevant market area, provided that the relocation not be at a site within 10 miles of a licensed new motor vehicle dealer for the same line make of motor vehicle. If this sub-subdivision is applicable, only dealers trading in the same line-make of vehicle that are located within the 10-mile radius shall be entitled to notice from the manufacturer and have the protest rights afforded under this section.

2. If the proposed additional new motor vehicle dealer is to be established at or within two miles of a location at which a former licensed new motor vehicle dealer for the same line make of new motor vehicle had ceased operating within the previous two years.

3. To the relocation of an existing new motor vehicle dealer within two miles of the existing site of the new motor vehicle dealership if the franchise has been operating on a regular basis from the existing site for a minimum of three years immediately preceding the relocation.

4. To the relocation of an existing new motor vehicle dealer if the proposed site of the relocated new motor vehicle dealership is further away from all other new motor vehicle dealers of the same line make in that relevant market area.

5. Repealed by Session Laws 2008-156, s. 3, effective August 3, 2008.

b. In determining whether good cause has been established for not entering into or relocating an additional new motor vehicle dealer for the same line make, the Commissioner shall take into consideration the existing circumstances, including, but not limited to:

1. The permanency of the investment of both the existing and proposed additional new motor vehicle dealers;

2. Growth or decline in population, density of population, and new car registrations in the relevant market area;

3. Effect on the consuming public in the relevant market area;

4. Whether it is injurious or beneficial to the public welfare for an additional new motor vehicle dealer to be established;

5. Whether the new motor vehicle dealers of the same line make in that relevant market area are providing adequate competition and convenient customer care for the motor vehicles of the same line make in the market area which shall include the adequacy of motor vehicle sales and service facilities, equipment, supply of motor vehicle parts, and qualified service personnel;

6. Whether the establishment of an additional new motor vehicle dealer or relocation of an existing new motor vehicle dealer in the relevant market area would increase competition in a manner such as to be in the long-term public interest; and

7. The effect on the relocating dealer of a denial of its relocation into the relevant market area.

c. The Commissioner shall try to conduct the hearing and render his final determination if possible, within 180 days after a protest is filed.

d. Any parties to a hearing by the Commissioner concerning the establishment or relocating of a new motor vehicle dealer shall have a right of review of the decision in a court of competent jurisdiction pursuant to Chapter 150B of the General Statutes.

e. In a hearing involving a proposed additional dealership, the manufacturer or distributor has the burden of proof under this section. In a proceeding involving the relocation of an existing dealership, the dealer seeking to relocate has the burden of proof under this section.

f. If the Commissioner determines, following a hearing, that good cause exists for permitting the proposed additional or relocated motor vehicle dealership, the dealer seeking the proposed additional or relocated motor vehicle dealership must, within two years, obtain a license from the Commissioner for the sale of vehicles at the relevant site, and actually commence operations at the site selling new motor vehicles of all line makes, as permitted by the Commissioner. Failure to obtain a permit and commence sales within two years shall constitute waiver by the dealer of the dealer's right to the additional or relocated dealership, requiring renotification, a new hearing, and a new determination as provided in this section. If the Commissioner fails to determine that good cause exists for permitting the proposed additional or relocated motor vehicle dealership, the manufacturer seeking the proposed additional dealership or dealer seeking to relocate may not again provide notice of its intention or otherwise attempt to establish an additional dealership or relocate to any location within 10 miles of the site of the original proposed additional dealership or relocation site for a minimum of three years from the date of the Commissioner's determination.

g. (See Editor's note for applicability) For purposes of this subdivision, the addition, creation, or operation of a "satellite" or other facility, not physically part of or contiguous to an existing licensed new motor vehicle dealer, whether or not owned or operated by a person or other entity holding a franchise as defined by G.S. 20-286(8a), at which warranty service work authorized or reimbursed by a manufacturer is performed or at which new motor vehicles are offered for sale to the public, shall be considered an additional new motor vehicle dealer requiring a showing of good cause, prior notification to existing new motor vehicle dealers of the same line make of vehicle within the relevant market area by the manufacturer and the opportunity for a hearing before the Commissioner as provided in this subdivision.

(6) Notwithstanding the terms, provisions or conditions of any franchise or notwithstanding the terms or provisions of any waiver, to terminate, cancel or fail to renew any franchise with a licensed new motor vehicle dealer unless the manufacturer has satisfied the notice requirements of subparagraph c. and the Commissioner has determined, if requested in writing by the dealer within (i) the time period specified in G.S. 20-305(6)c.1.II., III., or IV., as applicable, or (ii) the effective date of the franchise termination specified or proposed by the manufacturer in the notice of termination, whichever period of time is longer, and after a hearing on the matter, that there is good cause for the termination, cancellation, or nonrenewal of the franchise and that the manufacturer has acted in good faith as defined in this act regarding the termination, cancellation or nonrenewal. When such a petition is made to the Commissioner by a dealer for determination as to the existence of good cause and good faith for the termination, cancellation or nonrenewal of a franchise, the Commissioner shall promptly inform the manufacturer that a timely petition has been filed, and the franchise in question shall continue in effect pending the Commissioner's

decision. The Commissioner shall try to conduct the hearing and render a final determination within 180 days after a petition has been filed. If the termination, cancellation or nonrenewal is pursuant to G.S. 20-305(6)c.1.III. then the Commissioner shall give the proceeding priority consideration and shall try to render his final determination no later than 90 days after the petition has been filed. Any parties to a hearing by the Commissioner under this section shall have a right of review of the decision in a court of competent jurisdiction pursuant to Chapter 150B of the General Statutes. Any determination of the Commissioner under this section finding that good cause exists for the nonrenewal, cancellation, or termination of any franchise shall automatically be stayed during any period that the affected dealer shall have the right to judicial review or appeal of the determination before the superior court or any other appellate court and during the pendency of any appeal; provided, however, that within 30 days of entry of the Commissioner's order, the affected dealer provide such security as the reviewing court, in its discretion, may deem appropriate for payment of such costs and damages as may be incurred or sustained by the manufacturer by reason of and during the pendency of the stay. Although the right of the affected dealer to such stay is automatic, the procedure for providing such security and for the award of damages, if any, to the manufacturer upon dissolution of the stay shall be in accordance with G.S. 1A-1, Rule 65(d) and (e). No such security provided by or on behalf of any affected dealer shall be forfeited or damages awarded against a dealer who obtains a stay under this subdivision in the event the ownership of the affected dealership is subsequently transferred, sold, or assigned to a third party in accordance with this subdivision or subdivision (4) of this section and the closing on such transfer, sale, or assignment occurs no later than 180 days after the date of entry of the Commissioner's order. Furthermore, unless and until the termination, cancellation, or nonrenewal of a dealer's franchise shall finally become effective, in light of any stay or any order of the Commissioner determining that good cause exists for the termination, cancellation, or nonrenewal of a dealer's franchise as provided in this paragraph, a dealer who receives a notice of termination, cancellation, or nonrenewal from a manufacturer as provided in this subdivision shall continue to have the same rights to assign, sell, or transfer the franchise to a third party under the franchise and as permitted under G.S. 20-305(4) as if notice of the termination had not been given by the manufacturer. Any franchise under notice or threat of termination, cancellation, or nonrenewal by the manufacturer which is duly transferred in accordance with G.S. 20-305(4) shall not be subject to termination by reason of failure of performance or breaches of the franchise on the part of the transferor.

a. Notwithstanding the terms, provisions or conditions of any franchise or the terms or provisions of any waiver, good cause shall exist for the purposes of a termination, cancellation or nonrenewal when:

1. There is a failure by the new motor vehicle dealer to comply with a provision of the franchise which provision is both reasonable and of material significance to the franchise relationship provided that the dealer has been notified in writing of the failure within 180 days after the manufacturer first acquired knowledge of such failure;

2. If the failure by the new motor vehicle dealer relates to the performance of the new motor vehicle dealer in sales or service, then good cause shall be defined as the failure of the new motor vehicle dealer to comply with reasonable performance criteria established by the manufacturer if the new motor vehicle dealer was apprised by the manufacturer in writing of the failure; and

I. The notification stated that notice was provided of failure of performance pursuant to this section;

II. The new motor vehicle dealer was afforded a reasonable opportunity, for a period of not less than 180 days, to comply with the criteria; and

III. The new motor vehicle dealer failed to demonstrate substantial progress towards compliance with the manufacturer's performance criteria during such period and the new motor vehicle dealer's failure was not primarily due to economic or market factors within the dealer's relevant market area which were beyond the dealer's control.

b. The manufacturer shall have the burden of proof under this section.

c. Notification of Termination, Cancellation and Nonrenewal. -

1. Notwithstanding the terms, provisions or conditions of any franchise prior to the termination, cancellation or nonrenewal of any franchise, the manufacturer shall furnish notification of termination, cancellation or nonrenewal to the new motor vehicle dealer as follows:

I. In the manner described in G.S. 20-305(6)c2 below; and

II. Not less than 90 days prior to the effective date of such termination, cancellation or nonrenewal; or

III. Not less than 15 days prior to the effective date of such termination, cancellation or nonrenewal with respect to any of the following:

A. Insolvency of the new motor vehicle dealer, or filing of any petition by or against the new motor vehicle dealer under any bankruptcy or receivership law;

B. Failure of the new motor vehicle dealer to conduct its customary sales and service operations during its customary business hours for seven consecutive business days, except for acts of God or circumstances beyond the direct control of the new motor vehicle dealer;

C. Revocation of any license which the new motor vehicle dealer is required to have to operate a dealership;

D. Conviction of a felony involving moral turpitude, under the laws of this State or any other state, or territory, or the District of Columbia.

IV. Not less than 180 days prior to the effective date of such termination, cancellation, or nonrenewal which occurs as a result of any change in ownership, operation, or control of all or any part of the business of the manufacturer, factory branch, distributor, or distributor branch whether by sale or transfer of assets, corporate stock or other equity interest, assignment, merger, consolidation, combination, joint venture, redemption, operation of law or otherwise; or the termination, suspension, or cessation of a part or all of the business operations of the manufacturers, factory branch, distributor, or distributor branch; or discontinuance of the sale of the product line or a change in distribution system by the manufacturer whether through a change in distributors or the manufacturer's decision to cease conducting business through a distributor altogether.

V. Unless the failure by the new motor vehicle dealer relates to the performance of the new motor vehicle dealer in sales or service, not more than one year after the manufacturer first acquired knowledge of the basic facts comprising the failure.

2. Notification under this section shall be in writing; shall be by certified mail or personally delivered to the new motor vehicle dealer; and shall contain:

I. A statement of intention to terminate, cancel or not to renew the franchise;

II. A detailed statement of all of the material reasons for the termination, cancellation or nonrenewal; and

III. The date on which the termination, cancellation or nonrenewal takes effect.

3. Notification provided in G.S. 20-305(6)c1II of 90 days prior to the effective date of such termination, cancellation or renewal may run concurrent with the 180 days designated in G.S. 20-305(6)a2II provided the notification is clearly designated by a separate written document mailed by certified mail or personally delivered to the new motor vehicle dealer.

d. Payments.

1. Notwithstanding the terms of any franchise, agreement, or waiver, upon the termination, nonrenewal or cancellation of any franchise by the manufacturer or distributor, the cessation of business or the termination, nonrenewal, or cancellation of any franchise by any new motor vehicle dealer located in this State, or upon any of the occurrences set forth in G.S. 20-305(6)c.1.IV., the manufacturer or distributor shall purchase from and compensate the new motor vehicle dealer for all of the following:

I. Each new and unsold motor vehicle within the new motor vehicle dealer's inventory that has been acquired within 24 months of the effective date of the termination from the manufacturer or distributor or another same line-make dealer in the ordinary course of business, and which has not been substantially altered or damaged to the prejudice of the manufacturer or distributor while in the new motor vehicle dealer's possession, and which has been driven less than 1,000 miles or, for purposes of a recreational vehicle motor home as defined in G.S. 20-4.01(32a)a., less than 1,500 miles following the original date of delivery to the dealer, and for which no certificate of title has been issued. For purposes of this sub-subdivision, the term "ordinary course of business" shall include inventory transfers of all new, same line-make vehicles between affiliated dealerships, or otherwise between dealerships having common or interrelated ownership, provided that the transfer is not intended solely for the purpose of benefiting from the termination assistance described in this sub-subdivision.

II. Unused, undamaged and unsold supplies and parts purchased from the manufacturer or distributor or sources approved by the manufacturer or distributor, at a price not to exceed the original manufacturer's price to the dealer, provided such supplies and parts are currently offered for sale by the manufacturer or distributor in its current parts catalogs and are in salable condition.

III. Equipment, signs, and furnishings that have not been substantially altered or damaged and that have been required by the manufacturer or distributor to be purchased by the new motor vehicle dealer from the manufacturer or distributor, or their approved sources.

IV. Special tools that have not been altered or damaged, normal wear and tear excepted, and that have been required by the manufacturer or distributor to be purchased by the new motor vehicle dealer from the manufacturer or distributor, or their approved sources within five years immediately preceding the termination, nonrenewal or cancellation of the franchise. The amount of compensation which shall be paid to the new motor vehicle dealer by the manufacturer or distributor shall be the net acquisition price if the item was acquired in the 12 months preceding the date of receipt of the dealer's request for compensation; seventy-five percent (75%) of the net acquisition price if the item was acquired between 13 and 24 months preceding the dealer's request for compensation; fifty percent (50%) of the net acquisition price if the item was acquired between 25 and 36 months preceding the dealer's request for compensation; twenty-five percent (25%) of the net acquisition price if the item was acquired between 37 and 60 months preceding the dealer's request for compensation.

2. The compensation provided above shall be paid by the manufacturer or distributor not later than 90 days after the manufacturer or distributor has received notice in writing from or on behalf of the new motor vehicle dealer specifying the elements of compensation requested by the dealer; provided the new motor vehicle dealer has, or can obtain, clear title to the inventory and has conveyed, or can convey, title and possession of the same to the manufacturer or distributor. Within 15 days after receipt of the dealer's written request for compensation, the manufacturer or distributor shall send the dealer detailed written instructions and forms required by the manufacturer or distributor to effectuate the receipt of the compensation requested by the dealer. The manufacturer or distributor shall be obligated to pay or reimburse the dealer for any transportation charges associated with the repurchase obligations of the manufacturer or distributor under this sub-subparagraph. The manufacturer or distributor shall also compensate the dealer for any handling, packing, or similar payments contemplated in the franchise. In no event may the manufacturer or

distributor charge the dealer any handling, restocking, or other similar costs or fees associated with items repurchased by the manufacturer under this sub-subparagraph.

3. In addition to the other payments set forth in this section, if a termination, cancellation, or nonrenewal is premised upon any of the occurrences set forth in G.S. 20-305(6)c.1.IV., then the manufacturer or distributor shall be liable to the dealer for an amount at least equivalent to the fair market value of the franchise on (i) the date the franchisor announces the action which results in termination, cancellation, or nonrenewal; or (ii) the date the action which results in termination, cancellation, or nonrenewal first became general knowledge; or (iii) the day 18 months prior to the date on which the notice of termination, cancellation, or nonrenewal is issued, whichever amount is higher. Payment is due not later than 90 days after the manufacturer or distributor has received notice in writing from, or on behalf of, the new motor vehicle dealer specifying the elements of compensation requested by the dealer. If the termination, cancellation, or nonrenewal is due to a manufacturer's change in distributors, the manufacturer may avoid paying fair market value to the dealer if the new distributor or the manufacturer offers the dealer a franchise agreement with terms acceptable to the dealer.

e. Dealership Facilities Assistance upon Termination, Cancellation or Nonrenewal.

In the event of the occurrence of any of the events specified in G.S. 20-305(6)d.1. above, except termination, cancellation or nonrenewal for license revocation, conviction of a crime involving moral turpitude, or fraud by a dealer-owner:

1. Subject to paragraph 3, if the new motor vehicle dealer is leasing the dealership facilities from a lessor other than the manufacturer or distributor, the manufacturer or distributor shall pay the new motor vehicle dealer a sum equivalent to the rent for the unexpired term of the lease or three year's rent, whichever is less, or such longer term as is provided in the franchise agreement between the dealer and manufacturer; except that, in the case of motorcycle dealerships, the manufacturer shall pay the new motor vehicle dealer the sum equivalent to the rent for the unexpired term of the lease or one year's rent, whichever is less, or such longer term as provided in the franchise agreement between the dealer and manufacturer; or

2. Subject to paragraph 3, if the new motor vehicle dealer owns the dealership facilities, the manufacturer or distributor shall pay the new motor vehicle dealer a sum equivalent to the reasonable rental value of the dealership facilities for three years, or for one year in the case of motorcycle dealerships.

3. In order to be entitled to facilities assistance from the manufacturer or distributor, as provided in this paragraph e., the dealer, owner, or lessee, as the case may be, shall have the obligation to mitigate damages by listing the demised premises for lease or sublease with a licensed real estate agent within 30 days after the effective date of the termination of the franchise and thereafter by reasonably cooperating with said real estate agent in the performance of the agent's duties and responsibilities. In the event that the dealer, owner, or lessee is able to lease or sublease the demised premises, the dealer shall be obligated to pay the manufacturer the net revenue received from such mitigation up to the total amount of facilities assistance which the dealer has received from the manufacturer pursuant to sub-subdivisions 1. and 2. To the extent and for such uses and purposes as may be consistent with the terms of the lease, a manufacturer who pays facilities assistance to a dealer under this paragraph e. shall be entitled to occupy and use the dealership facilities during the years for which the manufacturer shall have paid rent under sub-subdivisions 1. and 2.

4. In the event the termination relates to fewer than all of the franchises operated by the dealer at a single location, the amount of facilities assistance which the manufacturer or distributor is required to pay the dealer under this sub-subdivision shall be based on the proportion of gross revenue received from the sale and lease of new vehicles by the dealer and from the dealer's parts and service operations during the three years immediately preceding the effective date of the termination (or any shorter period that the dealer may have held these franchises) of the line-makes being terminated, in relation to the gross revenue received from the sale and lease of all line-makes of new vehicles by the dealer and from the total of the dealer's and parts and service operations from this location during the same three-year period.

5. The compensation required for facilities assistance under this paragraph e. shall be paid by the manufacturer or distributor within 90 days after the manufacturer or distributor has received notice in writing from, or on behalf of, a new motor vehicle dealer specifying the elements of compensation requested by the dealer.

f. The provisions of sub-subdivision e. above shall not be applicable when the termination, nonrenewal, or cancellation of the franchise agreement by a new motor vehicle dealer is the result of the sale of assets or stock of the motor vehicle dealership. The provisions of sub-subdivisions d. and e. above shall not be applicable when the termination, nonrenewal, or cancellation of the franchise agreement is at the initiation of a new motor vehicle dealer of recreational vehicle motor homes, as defined in G.S. 20-4.01(32a)a., provided that at the time of the termination, nonrenewal, or cancellation, the recreational vehicle manufacturer or distributor has paid to the dealer all claims for warranty or recall work, including payments for labor, parts, and other expenses, which were submitted by the dealer 30 days or more prior to the date of termination, nonrenewal, or cancellation.

 g. A franchise shall continue in full force and operation notwithstanding a change, in whole or in part, of an established plan or system of distribution of the motor vehicles offered for sale under the franchise. The appointment of a new manufacturer, factory branch, distributor, or distributor branch for motor vehicles offered for sale under the franchise agreement shall be deemed to be a change of an established plan or system of distribution.

Upon the occurrence of the change, the Division shall deny an application of a manufacturer, factory branch, distributor, or distributor branch for a license or license renewal unless the applicant for a license as a manufacturer, factory branch, distributor, or distributor branch offers to each motor vehicle dealer who is a party to a franchise for that line-make a new franchise agreement containing substantially the same provisions which were contained in the previous franchise agreement or files an affidavit with the Division acknowledging its undertaking to assume and fulfill the rights, duties, and obligations of its predecessor under the previous franchise agreement.

 (7) Notwithstanding the terms of any contract or agreement, to prevent or refuse to honor the succession to a dealership, including the franchise, by a motor vehicle dealer's designated successor as provided for under this subsection.

 a. Any owner of a new motor vehicle dealership may appoint by will, or any other written instrument, a designated successor to succeed in the respective ownership interest or interest as principal operator of the owner in the new motor vehicle dealership, including the franchise, upon the death or incapacity of the owner or principal operator. In order for succession to the position of principal operator to occur by operation of law in accordance with sub-subdivision c. below, the owner's choice of a successor must be approved by the dealer, in accordance with the dealer's bylaws, if applicable, either prior or subsequent to the death or incapacity of the existing principal operator.

b. Any objections by a manufacturer or distributor to an owner's appointment of a designated successor shall be asserted in accordance with the following procedure:

1. Within 30 days after receiving written notice of the identity of the owner's designated successor and general information as to the financial ability and qualifications of the designated successor, the franchisor shall send the owner and designated successor notice of objection, by registered or certified mail, return receipt requested, to the appointment of the designated successor. The notice of objection shall state in detail all facts which constitute the basis for the contention on the part of the manufacturer or distributor that good cause, as defined in this sub-subdivision below, exists for rejection of the designated successor. Failure by the franchisor to send notice of objection within 30 days and otherwise as provided in this sub-subdivision shall constitute waiver by the franchisor of any right to object to the appointment of the designated successor.

2. Any time within 30 days of receipt of the manufacturer's notice of objection the owner or the designated successor may file a request in writing with the Commissioner that the Commissioner hold an evidentiary hearing and determine whether good cause exists for rejection of the designated successor. When such a request is filed, the Commissioner shall promptly inform the affected manufacturer or distributor that a timely request has been filed.

3. The Commissioner shall endeavor to hold the evidentiary hearing required under this sub-subdivision and render a determination within 180 days after receipt of the written request from the owner or designated successor. In determining whether good cause exists for rejection of the owner's appointed designated successor, the manufacturer or distributor has the burden of proving that the designated successor is a person who is not of good moral character or does not meet the franchisor's existing written and reasonable standards and, considering the volume of sales and service of the new motor vehicle dealer, uniformly applied minimum business experience standards in the market area.

4. Any parties to a hearing by the Commissioner concerning whether good cause exists for the rejection of the dealer's designated successor shall have a right of review of the decision in a court of competent jurisdiction pursuant to Chapter 150B of the General Statutes.

5. Nothing in this sub-subdivision shall preclude a manufacturer or distributor from, upon its receipt of written notice from an owner of the identity of the owner's designated successor, requiring that the designated successor promptly provide personal and financial data that is reasonably necessary to determine the financial ability and qualifications of the designated successor; provided, however, that such a request for additional information shall not delay any of the time periods or constraints contained herein.

6. In the event death or incapacity of the owner or principal operator occurs prior to the time a manufacturer or distributor receives notice of the owner's appointment of a designated successor or before the Commissioner has rendered a determination as provided above, the existing franchise shall remain in effect and the designated successor shall be deemed to have succeeded to all of the owner's or principal operator's rights and obligations in the dealership and under the franchise until a determination is made by the Commissioner or the rights of the parties have otherwise become fixed in accordance with this sub-subdivision.

c. Except as otherwise provided in sub-subdivision d. of this subdivision, any designated successor of a deceased or incapacitated owner or principal operator of a new motor vehicle dealership appointed by such owner in substantial compliance with this section shall, by operation of law, succeed at the time of such death or incapacity to all of the rights and obligations of the owner or principal operator in the new motor vehicle dealership and under either the existing franchise or any other successor, renewal, or replacement franchise.

d. Within 60 days after the death or incapacity of the owner or principal operator, a designated successor appointed in substantial compliance with this section shall give the affected manufacturer or distributor written notice of his or her succession to the position of owner or principal operator of the new motor vehicle dealership; provided, however, that the failure of the designated successor to give the manufacturer or distributor written notice as provided above within 60 days of the death or incapacity of the owner or principal operator shall not result in the waiver or termination of the designated successor's right to succeed to the ownership of the new motor vehicle dealership unless the manufacturer or distributor gives written notice of this provision to either the designated successor or the deceased or incapacitated owner's executor, administrator, guardian or other fiduciary by certified or registered mail, return receipt requested, and said written notice grants not less than 30 days time within which the designated successor may give the notice required hereunder, provided the designated successor or the deceased or incapacitated owner's executor, administrator, guardian or other fiduciary has given the manufacturer reasonable notice of death or incapacity. Within 30 days of receipt of the notice by the manufacturer or distributor from the designated successor provided in this paragraph, the manufacturer or distributor may request that the designated successor complete the application forms generally utilized by the manufacturer or distributor to review the designated successor's qualifications to establish a successor dealership. Within 30 days of receipt of the completed forms, the manufacturer or distributor shall send a letter by certified or registered mail, return receipt requested, advising the designated successor of facts and circumstances which have changed since the manufacturer's or distributor's original approval of the designated successor, and which have caused the manufacturer or distributor to object to the designated successor. Upon receipt of such notice, the designated successor may either designate an alternative successor or may file a request for evidentiary hearing in accordance with the procedures provided in sub-subdivisions b. 2. -5. of this subdivision. In any such hearing, the manufacturer or distributor shall be limited to facts and circumstances which did not exist at the time the designated successor was originally approved or evidence which was originally requested to be produced by the designated successor at the time of the original request and was fraudulent.

e. The designated successor shall agree to be bound by all terms and conditions of the franchise in effect between the manufacturer or distributor and the owner at the time of the owner's or principal operator's death or incapacity, if so requested in writing by the manufacturer or distributor subsequent to the owner's or principal operator's death or incapacity.

f. This section does not preclude an owner of a new motor vehicle dealership from designating any person as his or her successor by written instrument filed with the manufacturer or distributor, and, in the event there is an inconsistency between the successor named in such written instrument and the designated successor otherwise appointed by the owner consistent with the provisions of this section, and that written instrument has not been revoked by the owner of the new motor vehicle dealership in writing to the manufacturer or distributor, then the written instrument filed with the manufacturer or distributor shall govern as to the appointment of the successor.

(8) To require, coerce, or attempt to coerce any new motor vehicle dealer in this State to order or accept delivery of any new motor vehicle with special

features, accessories or equipment not included in the list price of those motor vehicles as publicly advertised by the manufacturer or distributor.

(9)   To require, coerce, or attempt to coerce any new motor vehicle dealer in this State to purchase nondiagnostic computer equipment or programs, to participate monetarily in an advertising campaign or contest, or to purchase unnecessary or unreasonable quantities of any promotional materials, training materials, training programs, showroom or other display decorations, materials, computer equipment or programs, or special tools at the expense of the new motor vehicle dealer, provided that nothing in this subsection shall preclude a manufacturer or distributor from including an unitemized uniform charge in the base price of the new motor vehicle charged to the dealer where such charge is attributable to advertising costs incurred or to be incurred by the manufacturer or distributor in the ordinary courses of its business.

(10)   To require, coerce, or attempt to coerce any new motor vehicle dealer in this State to change the capital structure of the new motor vehicle dealer or the means by or through which the new motor vehicle dealer finances the operation of the dealership provided that the new motor vehicle dealer at all times meets any reasonable capital standards determined by the manufacturer in accordance with uniformly applied criteria; and also provided that no change in the capital structure shall cause a change in the principal management or have the effect of a sale of the franchise without the consent of the manufacturer or distributor, provided that said consent shall not be unreasonably withheld.

(11)   To require, coerce, or attempt to coerce any new motor vehicle dealer in this State to refrain from participation in the management of, investment in, or the acquisition of any other line of new motor vehicle or related products; Provided, however, that this subsection does not apply unless the new motor vehicle dealer maintains a reasonable line of credit for each make or line of new motor vehicle, and the new motor vehicle dealer remains in compliance with any reasonable capital standards and facilities requirements of the manufacturer. The reasonable facilities requirements shall not include any requirement that a new motor vehicle dealer establish or maintain exclusive facilities, personnel, or display space.

(12)   To require, coerce, or attempt to coerce any new motor vehicle dealer in this State to change location of the dealership, or to make any substantial alterations to the dealership premises or facilities, when to do so would be unreasonable, or without written assurance of a sufficient supply of new motor

vehicles so as to justify such an expansion, in light of the current market and economic conditions.

(13) To require, coerce, or attempt to coerce any new motor vehicle dealer in this State to prospectively assent to a release, assignment, novation, waiver or estoppel which would relieve any person from liability to be imposed by this law or to require any controversy between a new motor vehicle dealer and a manufacturer, distributor, or representative, to be referred to any person other than the duly constituted courts of the State or the United States of America, or to the Commissioner, if such referral would be binding upon the new motor vehicle dealer.

(14) To delay, refuse, or fail to deliver motor vehicles or motor vehicle parts or accessories in reasonable quantities relative to the new motor vehicle dealer's facilities and sales potential in the new motor vehicle dealer's market area as determined in accordance with reasonably applied economic principles, or within a reasonable time, after receipt of an order from a dealer having a franchise for the retail sale of any new motor vehicle sold or distributed by the manufacturer or distributor, any new vehicle, parts or accessories to new vehicles as are covered by such franchise, and such vehicles, parts or accessories as are publicly advertised as being available or actually being delivered. The delivery to another dealer of a motor vehicle of the same model and similarly equipped as the vehicle ordered by a motor vehicle dealer who has not received delivery thereof, but who has placed his written order for the vehicle prior to the order of the dealer receiving the vehicle, shall be evidence of a delayed delivery of, or refusal to deliver, a new motor vehicle to a motor vehicle dealer within a reasonable time, without cause. Additionally, except as may be required by any consent decree of the Commissioner or other order of the Commissioner or court of competent jurisdiction, any sales objectives which a manufacturer, factory branch, distributor, or distributor branch establishes for any of its franchised dealers in this State must be reasonable, and every manufacturer, factory branch, distributor, or distributor branch must allocate its products within this State in a manner that does all of the following:

a. Provides each of its franchised dealers in this State an adequate supply of vehicles by series, product line, and model in a fair, reasonable, and equitable manner based on each dealer's historical selling pattern and reasonable sales standards as compared to other same line-make dealers in the State.

b. Allocates an adequate supply of vehicles to each of its dealers by series, product line, and model so as to allow the dealer to achieve any performance standards established by the manufacturer and distributor.

c. Is fair and equitable to all of its franchised dealers in this State.

d. Makes available to each of its franchised dealers in this State a minimum of one of each vehicle series, model, or product line that the manufacturer makes available to any dealer in this State and advertises in the State as being available for purchase.

e. Does not unfairly discriminate among its franchised dealers in its allocation process.

This subsection is not violated, however, if such failure is caused solely by the occurrence of temporary international, national, or regional product shortages resulting from natural disasters, unavailability of parts, labor strikes, product recalls, and other factors and events beyond the control of the manufacturer that temporarily reduce a manufacturer's product supply. The willful or malicious maintenance, creation, or alteration of a vehicle allocation process or formula by a manufacturer, factory branch, distributor, or distributor branch that is in any part designed or intended to force or coerce a dealer in this State to close or sell the dealer's franchise, cause the dealer financial distress, or to relocate, update, or renovate the dealer's existing dealership facility shall constitute an unfair and deceptive trade practice under G.S. 75-1.1.

(15) To refuse to disclose to any new motor vehicle dealer, handling the same line make, the manner and mode of distribution of that line make within the State.

(16) To award money, goods, services, or any other benefit to any new motor vehicle dealership employee, either directly or indirectly, unless such benefit is promptly accounted for, and transmitted to, or approved by, the new motor vehicle dealer.

(17) To increase prices of new motor vehicles which the new motor vehicle dealer had ordered and which the manufacturer or distributor has accepted for immediate delivery for private retail consumers prior to the new motor vehicle dealer's receipt of the written official price increase notification. A sales contract signed by a private retail consumer shall constitute evidence of each such order provided that the vehicle is in fact delivered to that customer. Price differences

applicable to new model or series shall not be considered a price increase or price decrease. Price changes caused by either: (i) the addition to a new motor vehicle of required or optional equipment; or (ii) revaluation of the United States dollar, in the case of foreign-make vehicles or components; or (iii) an increase in transportation charges due to increased rates imposed by carriers; or (iv) new tariffs or duties imposed by the United States of America or any other governmental authority, shall not be subject to the provisions of this subsection.

(18) To prevent or attempt to prevent a dealer from receiving fair and reasonable compensation for the value of the franchised business transferred in accordance with G.S. 20-305(4) above, or to prevent or attempt to prevent, through the exercise of any contractual right of first refusal or otherwise, a dealer located in this State from transferring the franchised business to such persons or other entities as the dealer shall designate in accordance with G.S. 20-305(4). The opinion or determination of a manufacturer that the existence or location of one of its franchised dealers situated in this State is not viable or is not consistent with the manufacturer's distribution or marketing forecast or plans shall not constitute a lawful basis for the manufacturer to fail or refuse to approve a dealer's proposed transfer of ownership submitted in accordance with G.S. 20-305(4), or "good cause" for the termination, cancellation, or nonrenewal of the franchise under G.S. 20-305(6) or grounds for the objection to an owner's designated successor appointed pursuant to G.S. 20-305(7).

(19) To offer any refunds or other types of inducements to any person for the purchase of new motor vehicles of a certain line make to be sold to the State or any political subdivision thereof without making the same offer available upon request to all other new motor vehicle dealers in the same line make within the State.

(20) To release to any outside party, except under subpoena or as otherwise required by law or in an administrative, judicial or arbitration proceeding involving the manufacturer or new motor vehicle dealer, any confidential business, financial, or personal information which may be from time to time provided by the new motor vehicle dealer to the manufacturer, without the express written consent of the new motor vehicle dealer.

(21) To deny any new motor vehicle dealer the right of free association with any other new motor vehicle dealer for any lawful purpose.

(22) To unfairly discriminate among its new motor vehicle dealers with respect to warranty reimbursements or authority granted its new motor vehicle dealers to make warranty adjustments with retail customers.

(23) To engage in any predatory practice against or unfairly compete with a new motor vehicle dealer located in this State.

(24) To terminate any franchise solely because of the death or incapacity of an owner who is not listed in the franchise as one on whose expertise and abilities the manufacturer relied in the granting of the franchise.

(25) To require, coerce, or attempt to coerce a new motor vehicle dealer in this State to either establish or maintain exclusive facilities, personnel, or display space.

(26) To resort to or to use any false or misleading advertisement in the conducting of its business as a manufacturer or distributor in this State.

(27) To knowingly make, either directly or through any agent or employee, any material statement which is false or misleading or conceal any material facts which induce any new motor vehicle dealer to enter into any agreement or franchise or to take any action which is materially prejudicial to that new motor vehicle dealer or his business.

(28) To require, coerce, or attempt to coerce any new motor vehicle dealer to purchase or order any new motor vehicle as a precondition to purchasing, ordering, or receiving any other new motor vehicle or vehicles. Nothing herein shall prevent a manufacturer from requiring that a new motor vehicle dealer fairly represent and inventory the full line of current model year new motor vehicles which are covered by the franchise agreement, provided that such inventory representation requirements are not unreasonable under the circumstances.

(29) To require, coerce, or attempt to coerce any new motor vehicle dealer to sell, transfer, or otherwise issue stock or other ownership interest in the dealership corporation to a general manager or any other person involved in the management of the dealership other than the dealer principal or dealer operator named in the franchise, unless the dealer principal or dealer operator is an absentee owner who is not involved in the operation of the dealership on a regular basis.

(30) To vary the price charged to any of its franchised new motor vehicle dealers located in this State for new motor vehicles based on the dealer's purchase of new facilities, supplies, tools, equipment, or other merchandise from the manufacturer, the dealer's relocation, remodeling, repair, or renovation of existing dealerships or construction of a new facility, the dealer's participation in training programs sponsored, endorsed, or recommended by the manufacturer, whether or not the dealer is dualed with one or more other line makes of new motor vehicles, or the dealer's sales penetration. Except as provided in this subdivision, it shall be unlawful for any manufacturer, factory branch, distributor, or distributor branch, or any field representative, officer, agent, or any representative whatsoever of any of them to vary the price charged to any of its franchised new motor vehicle dealers located in this State for new motor vehicles based on the dealer's sales volume, the dealer's level of sales or customer service satisfaction, the dealer's purchase of advertising materials, signage, nondiagnostic computer hardware or software, communications devices, or furnishings, or the dealer's participation in used motor vehicle inspection or certification programs sponsored or endorsed by the manufacturer.

The price of the vehicle, for purposes of this subdivision shall include the manufacturer's use of rebates, credits, or other consideration that has the effect of causing a variance in the price of new motor vehicles offered to its franchised dealers located in the State.

Notwithstanding the foregoing, nothing in this subdivision shall be deemed to preclude a manufacturer from establishing sales contests or promotions that provide or award dealers or consumers rebates or incentives; provided, however, that the manufacturer complies with all of the following conditions:

a. With respect to manufacturer to consumer rebates and incentives, the manufacturer's criteria for determining eligibility shall:

1. Permit all of the manufacturer's franchised new motor vehicle dealers in this State to offer the rebate or incentive; and

2. Be uniformly applied and administered to all eligible consumers.

b. With respect to manufacturer to dealer rebates and incentives, the rebate or incentive program shall:

1. Be based solely on the dealer's actual or reasonably anticipated sales volume or on a uniform per vehicle sold or leased basis;

2. Be uniformly available, applied, and administered to all of the manufacturer's franchised new motor vehicle dealers in this State; and

3. Provide that any of the manufacturer's franchised new motor vehicle dealers in this State may, upon written request, obtain the method or formula used by the manufacturer in establishing the sales volumes for receiving the rebates or incentives and the specific calculations for determining the required sales volumes of the inquiring dealer and any of the manufacturer's other franchised new motor vehicle dealers located within 75 miles of the inquiring dealer.

Nothing contained in this subdivision shall prohibit a manufacturer from providing assistance or encouragement to a franchised dealer to remodel, renovate, recondition, or relocate the dealer's existing facilities, provided that this assistance, encouragement, or rewards are not determined on a per vehicle basis.

It is unlawful for any manufacturer to charge or include the cost of any program or policy prohibited under this subdivision in the price of new motor vehicles that the manufacturer sells to its franchised dealers or purchasers located in this State.

In the event that as of October 1, 1999, a manufacturer was operating a program that varied the price charged to its franchised dealers in this State in a manner that would violate this subdivision, or had in effect a documented policy that had been conveyed to its franchised dealers in this State and that varied the price charged to its franchised dealers in this State in a manner that would violate this subdivision, it shall be lawful for that program or policy, including amendments to that program or policy that are consistent with the purpose and provisions of the existing program or policy, or a program or policy similar thereto implemented after October 1, 1999, to continue in effect as to the manufacturer's franchised dealers located in this State until June 30, 2018.

In the event that as of June 30, 2001, a manufacturer was operating a program that varied the price charged to its franchised dealers in this State in a manner that would violate this subdivision, or had in effect a documented policy that had been conveyed to its franchised dealers in this State and that varied the price charged to its franchised dealers in this State in a manner that would violate this subdivision, and the program or policy was implemented in this State subsequent to October 1, 1999, and prior to June 30, 2001, and provided that the program or policy is in compliance with this subdivision as it existed as of June 30, 2001, it shall be lawful for that program or policy, including amendments to that program or policy that comply with this subdivision as it existed as of June 30, 2001, to continue in effect as to the manufacturer's franchised dealers located in this State until June 30, 2018.

Any manufacturer shall be required to pay or otherwise compensate any franchise dealer who has earned the right to receive payment or other compensation under a program in accordance with the manufacturer's program or policy.

The provisions of this subdivision shall not be applicable to multiple or repeated sales of new motor vehicles made by a new motor vehicle dealer to a single purchaser under a bona fide fleet sales policy of a manufacturer, factory branch, distributor, or distributor branch.

(31)   Notwithstanding the terms of any contract, franchise, agreement, release, or waiver, to require that in any civil or administrative proceeding in which a new motor vehicle dealer asserts any claims, rights, or defenses arising under this Article or under the franchise, that the dealer or any nonprevailing party compensate the manufacturer or prevailing party for any court costs, attorneys' fees, or other expenses incurred in the litigation.

(32)   To require that any of its franchised new motor vehicle dealers located in this State pay any extra fee, purchase unreasonable or unnecessary quantities of advertising displays or other materials, or remodel, renovate, or recondition the dealers' existing facilities in order to receive any particular model or series of vehicles manufactured or distributed by the manufacturer for which the dealers have a valid franchise. Notwithstanding the foregoing, nothing contained in this subdivision shall be deemed to prohibit or prevent a manufacturer from requiring that its franchised dealers located in this State purchase special tools or equipment, stock reasonable quantities of certain parts, or participate in training programs which are reasonably necessary for those dealers to sell or service any model or series of vehicles.

(33)   To fail to reimburse a dealer located in this State in full for the actual cost of providing a loaner vehicle to any customer who is having a vehicle serviced at the dealership if the provision of such a loaner vehicle is required by the manufacturer.

(34) To require, coerce, or attempt to coerce any new motor vehicle dealer in this State to participate monetarily in any training program whose subject matter is not expressly limited to specific information necessary to sell or service the models of vehicles the dealer is authorized to sell or service under the dealer's franchise with that manufacturer. Examples of training programs with respect to which a manufacturer is prohibited from requiring the dealer's monetary participation include, but are not limited to, those which purport to teach morale-boosting employee motivation, teamwork, or general principles of customer relations. A manufacturer is further prohibited from requiring the personal attendance of an owner or dealer principal of any dealership located in this State at any meeting or training program at which it is reasonably possible for another member of the dealer's management to attend and later relate the subject matter of the meeting or training program to the dealership's owners or principal operator.

(35) Notwithstanding the terms of any franchise, agreement, waiver or novation, to limit the number of franchises of the same line make of vehicle that any franchised motor vehicle dealer, including its parent(s), subsidiaries, and affiliates, if any, may own or operate or attach any restrictions or conditions on the ownership or operation of multiple franchises of the same line make of motor vehicle without making the same limitations, conditions, and restrictions applicable to all of its other franchisees.

(36) With regard to any manufacturer, factory branch, distributor, distributor branch, or subsidiary thereof that owns and operates a new motor vehicle dealership, directly or indirectly through any subsidiary or affiliated entity as provided in G.S. 20-305.2, to unreasonably discriminate against any other new motor vehicle dealer in the same line make in any matter governed by the motor vehicle franchise, including the sale or allocation of vehicles or other manufacturer or distributor products, or the execution of dealer programs for benefits.

(37) Subdivisions (11) and (25) of this section shall not apply to any manufacturer, manufacturer branch, distributor, distributor branch, or any affiliate or subsidiary thereof of new motor vehicles which manufactures or distributes exclusively new motor vehicles with a gross weight rating of 8,500 pounds or more, provided that the following conditions are met: (i) the manufacturer has, as of November 1, 1996, an agreement in effect with at least three of its franchised dealers within the State, and which agreement was, in fact, being enforced by the manufacturer, requiring the dealers to maintain

separate and exclusive facilities for the vehicles it manufactures or distributes; and (ii) there existed at least seven dealerships (locations) of that manufacturer within the State as of January 1, 1999.

(38)   Notwithstanding the terms, provisions, or conditions of any agreement, franchise, novation, waiver, or other written instrument, to assign or change a franchised new motor vehicle dealer's area of responsibility under the franchise arbitrarily or without due regard to the present or projected future pattern of motor vehicle sales and registrations within the dealer's market and without having provided the affected dealer with written notice of the change in the dealer's area of responsibility and a detailed description of the change in writing by registered or certified mail, return receipt requested. A franchised new motor vehicle dealer who believes that a manufacturer, factory branch, distributor, or distributor branch with whom the dealer has entered into a franchise has violated this subdivision may file a petition before the Commissioner as provided in G.S. 20-301(b) contesting the franchised new motor vehicle dealer's assigned area of responsibility. At the hearing before the Commissioner, the affected manufacturer, factory branch, distributor, or distributor branch shall have the burden of proving that all portions of its current or proposed area of responsibility for the petitioning franchised new motor vehicle dealer are reasonable in light of the present or projected future pattern of motor vehicle sales and registrations within the franchised new motor vehicle dealer's market. If a protest is or has been filed under G.S. 20-305(5) and the franchised new motor vehicle dealer's area of responsibility is included in the relevant market area under the protest, any protest filed under this subdivision shall be consolidated with that protest for hearing and joint disposition of all of the protests.

(39)   Notwithstanding the terms, provisions, or conditions of any agreement, franchise, novation, waiver, or other written instrument, to require, coerce, or attempt to coerce any of its franchised motor vehicle dealers in this State to purchase, lease, erect, or relocate one or more signs displaying the name of the manufacturer or franchised motor vehicle dealer upon unreasonable or onerous terms or conditions or if installation of the additional signage would violate local signage or zoning laws to which the franchised motor vehicle dealer is subject. Any term, provision, or condition of any agreement, franchise, waiver, novation, or any other written instrument which is in violation of this subdivision shall be deemed null and void and without force and effect.

(40)   Notwithstanding the terms, provisions, or conditions of any agreement or franchise, to require any dealer to floor plan any of the dealer's inventory or

finance the acquisition, construction, or renovation of any of the dealer's property or facilities by or through any financial source or sources designated by the manufacturer, factory branch, distributor, or distributor branch, including any financial source or sources that is or are directly or indirectly owned, operated, or controlled by the manufacturer, factory branch, distributor, or distributor branch.

(41)   Notwithstanding the terms, provisions, or conditions of any agreement or franchise, to use or consider the performance of any of its franchised new motor vehicle dealers located in this State relating to the sale of the manufacturer's new motor vehicles or ability to satisfy any minimum sales or market share quota or responsibility relating to the sale of the manufacturer's new motor vehicles in determining:

a.   The dealer's eligibility to purchase program, certified, or other used motor vehicles from the manufacturer;

b.   The volume, type, or model of program, certified, or other used motor vehicles the dealer shall be eligible to purchase from the manufacturer;

c.   The price or prices of any program, certified, or other used motor vehicles that the dealer shall be eligible to purchase from the manufacturer; or

d.   The availability or amount of any discount, credit, rebate, or sales incentive the dealer shall be eligible to receive from the manufacturer for the purchase of any program, certified, or other used motor vehicles offered for sale by the manufacturer.

(42)   Notwithstanding the terms, provisions, or conditions of any agreement or waiver, to directly or indirectly condition the awarding of a franchise to a prospective new motor vehicle dealer, the addition of a line make or franchise to an existing dealer, the renewal of a franchise of an existing dealer, the approval of the relocation of an existing dealer's facility, or the approval of the sale or transfer of the ownership of a franchise on the willingness of a dealer, proposed new dealer, or owner of an interest in the dealership facility to enter into a site control agreement or exclusive use agreement. For purposes of this subdivision, the terms "site control agreement" and "exclusive use agreement" include any agreement that has the effect of either: (i) requiring that the dealer establish or maintain exclusive dealership facilities; or (ii) restricting the ability of the dealer, or the ability of the dealer's lessor in the event the dealership facility is being leased, to transfer, sell, lease, or change the use of the dealership premises,

whether by sublease, lease, collateral pledge of lease, right of first refusal to purchase or lease, option to purchase, option to lease, or other similar agreement, regardless of the parties to such agreement. Any provision contained in any agreement entered into on or after August 26, 2009, that is inconsistent with the provisions of this subdivision shall be voidable at the election of the affected dealer, prospective dealer, or owner of an interest in the dealership facility.

(43) Notwithstanding the terms, provisions, or conditions of any agreement, franchise, novation, waiver, or other written instrument, to require, coerce, or attempt to coerce any of its franchised motor vehicle dealers in this State to change the principal operator, general manager, or any other manager or supervisor employed by the dealer. Any term, provision, or condition of any agreement, franchise, waiver, novation, or any other written instrument that is inconsistent with this subdivision shall be deemed null and void and without force and effect.

(44) Notwithstanding the terms, provisions, or conditions of any agreement or franchise, to require, coerce, or attempt to coerce any new motor vehicle dealer located in this State to refrain from displaying in the dealer's showroom or elsewhere within the dealership facility any sports-related honors, awards, photographs, displays, or other artifacts or memorabilia; provided, however, that such sports-related honors, awards, photographs, displays, or other artifacts or memorabilia (i) pertain to an owner, investor, or executive manager of the dealership; (ii) relate to professional sports; (iii) do not reference or advertise a competing brand of motor vehicles; and (iv) do not conceal or disparage any of the required branding elements that are part of the dealership facility.

(45) Nothwithstanding the terms, provisions, or conditions of any agreement or franchise, to discriminate against a new motor vehicle dealer located in this State for selling or offering for sale a service contract, debt cancellation agreement, maintenance agreement, or similar product not approved, endorsed, sponsored, or offered by the manufacturer, distributor, affiliate, or captive finance source. For purposes of this subdivision, discrimination includes any of the following:

a. Requiring or coercing a dealer to exclusively sell or offer for sale service contracts, debt cancellation agreements, or similar products approved, endorsed, sponsored, or offered by the manufacturer, distributor, affiliate, or captive finance source.

b. Taking or threatening to take any adverse action against a dealer (i) because the dealer sells or offers for sale any service contracts, debt cancellation agreements, maintenance agreements, or similar products that have not been approved, endorsed, sponsored, or offered by the manufacturer, distributor, affiliate, or captive finance source or (ii) because the dealer fails to sell or offer for sale service contracts, debt cancellation agreements, maintenance agreements, or similar products approved, endorsed, sponsored, or offered by the manufacturer, distributor, their affiliate, or captive finance source.

c. Measuring a dealer's performance under a franchise in any part based upon the dealer's sale of service contracts, debt cancellation agreements, or similar products approved, endorsed, sponsored, or offered by the manufacturer, distributor, affiliate, or captive finance source.

d. Requiring a dealer to exclusively promote the sale of service contracts, debt cancellation agreements, or similar products approved, endorsed, sponsored, or offered by the manufacturer, distributor, affiliate, or captive finance source.

e. Considering the dealer's sale of service contracts, debt cancellation agreements, or similar products approved, endorsed, sponsored, or offered by the manufacturer, distributor, affiliate, or captive finance source in determining any of the following:

1. The dealer's eligibility to purchase any vehicles, parts, or other products or services from the manufacturer or distributor.

2. The volume of vehicles or other parts or services the dealer shall be eligible to purchase from the manufacturer or distributor.

3. The price or prices of any vehicles, parts, or other products or services that the dealer shall be eligible to purchase from the manufacturer or distributor.

4. The availability or amount of any vehicle discount, credit, special pricing, rebate, or sales or service incentive the dealer shall be eligible to receive from the manufacturer, distributor, affiliate, or captive finance source in which the incentives are calculated or paid on a per-vehicle basis or any vehicle discount, credit, special pricing, or rebate that are calculated or paid on a per-vehicle basis.

For purposes of this subdivision, discrimination does not include, and nothing shall prohibit a manufacturer, distributor, affiliate, or captive finance source from, offering discounts, rebates, or other incentives to dealers who voluntarily sell or offer for sale service contracts, debt cancellation agreements, or similar products approved, endorsed, sponsored, or offered by the manufacturer, distributor, affiliate, or captive finance source; provided, however, that such discounts, rebates, or other incentives are based solely on the sales volume of the service contracts, debt cancellation agreements, or similar products sold by the dealer and do not provide vehicle sales or service incentives.

For purposes of this subdivision, a service contract provider or its representative shall not complete any sale or transaction of an extended service contract, extended maintenance plan, or similar product using contract forms that do not disclose the identity of the service contract provider.

(46) To require, coerce, or attempt to coerce a dealer located in this State to purchase goods or services of any nature from a vendor selected, identified, or designated by a manufacturer, distributor, affiliate, or captive finance source when the dealer may obtain goods or services of substantially similar quality and design from a vendor selected by the dealer, provided the dealer obtains prior approval from the manufacturer, distributor, affiliate, or captive finance source, for the use of the dealer's selected vendor. Such approval by the manufacturer, distributor, affiliate, or captive finance source may not be unreasonably withheld. For purposes of this subdivision, the term "goods" does not include moveable displays, brochures, and promotional materials containing material subject to the intellectual property rights of a manufacturer or distributor, or special tools as reasonably required by the manufacturer, or parts to be used in repairs under warranty obligations of a manufacturer or distributor. If the manufacturer, distributor, affiliate, or captive finance source claims that a vendor chosen by the dealer cannot supply goods and services of substantially similar quality and design, the dealer may file a protest with the Commissioner. When a protest is filed, the Commissioner shall promptly inform the manufacturer, distributor, affiliate, or captive finance source that a protest has been filed. The Commissioner shall conduct a hearing on the merits of the protest within 90 days following the filing of a response to the protest. The manufacturer, distributor, affiliate, or captive finance source shall bear the burden of proving that the goods or services chosen by the dealer are not of substantially similar quality and design to those required by the manufacturer, distributor, affiliate, or captive finance source.

(47) To fail to provide to a dealer, if the goods or services to be supplied to the dealer by a vendor selected, identified, or designated by the manufacturer or distributor are signs or other franchisor image elements to be purchased or leased to the dealer, the right to purchase or lease the signs or other franchisor image elements of similar quality and design from a vendor selected by the dealer. This subdivision and subdivision (46) of this section shall not be construed to allow a dealer or vendor to violate directly or indirectly the intellectual property rights of the manufacturer or distributor, including, but not limited to, the manufacturer's or distributor's intellectual property rights in any trademarks or trade dress, or other intellectual property interests owned or controlled by the manufacturer or distributor, or to permit a dealer to erect or maintain signs that do not conform to the reasonable intellectual property right or trademark and trade dress usage guidelines of the manufacturer or distributor.

(48) To unreasonably interfere with a dealer's independence in staffing the dealership by engaging in any of the following conduct: (i) requiring, coercing, or attempting to coerce a dealer located in this State to employ, appoint, or designate an individual to serve full-time or exclusively in any specific capacity, role, or job function at the dealership, other than the employment or appointment of a full-time general manager; (ii) requiring a dealer to employ, appoint, or designate an individual to serve full-time or exclusively in any specific capacity, role, or job function at the dealership, other than the employment or appointment of a full-time general manager, in order to participate in or qualify for any incentive program offered or sponsored by the manufacturer or distributor or to otherwise receive any discounts, credits, rebates, or incentives of any kind that are calculated or paid on a per-vehicle basis; or (iii) requiring that the dealer obtain the approval of the manufacturer or distributor prior to employing or appointing any individual in any capacity, role, or job function at the dealership, other than the employment or appointment of a full-time general manager. Except as expressly provided above, nothing contained in this subdivision shall be deemed to prevent or prohibit a manufacturer or distributor from requiring that a dealer employ a reasonable number of trained employees to sell and service the factory's vehicles. (1955, c. 1243, s. 21; 1973, c. 88, ss. 1, 2; 1983, c. 704, ss. 5-10; 1987, c. 827, s. 1; 1991, c. 510, ss. 2-4; 1993, c. 123, s. 1; c. 331, s. 2; 1995, c. 163, s. 13; c. 480, s. 3; 1997-319, s. 3; 1999-335, s. 2; 1999-336, s. 1; 2001-510, ss. 2, 6; 2003-113, ss. 2, 3, 4; 2005-409, s. 2; 2005-463, s. 2; 2007-513, ss. 2-4, 9, 12; 2008-156, s. 3; 2008-187, s. 50; 2009-338, ss. 1, 2, 5; 2009-496, s. 1; 2011-290, ss. 5-9; 2013-302, s. 7.)

§ 20-305.1. Automobile dealer warranty obligations.

(a) Each motor vehicle manufacturer, factory branch, distributor or distributor branch, shall specify in writing to each of its motor vehicle dealers licensed in this State the dealer's obligations for preparation, delivery and warranty service on its products, the schedule of compensation to be paid such dealers for parts, work, and service in connection with warranty service, and the time allowances for the performance of such work and service. In no event shall such schedule of compensation fail to include reasonable compensation for diagnostic work and associated administrative requirements as well as repair service and labor. Time allowances for the performance of warranty work and service shall be reasonable and adequate for the work to be performed. The compensation which must be paid under this section must be reasonable, provided, however, that under no circumstances may the reasonable compensation under this section be in an amount less than the dealer's current retail labor rate and the amount charged to retail customers for the manufacturer's or distributor's original parts for nonwarranty work of like kind, provided such amount is competitive with the retail rates charged for parts and labor by other franchised dealers within the dealer's market.

(a1) The retail rate customarily charged by the dealer for parts and labor may be established at the election of the dealer by the dealer submitting to the manufacturer or distributor 100 sequential nonwarranty customer-paid service repair orders which contain warranty-like parts, or 60 consecutive days of nonwarranty customer-paid service repair orders which contain warranty-like parts, whichever is less, covering repairs made no more than 180 days before the submission and declaring the average percentage markup. The average of the parts markup rate and the average labor rate shall both be presumed to be reasonable, however, a manufacturer or distributor may, not later than 30 days after submission, rebut that presumption by reasonably substantiating that the rate is unfair and unreasonable in light of the retail rates charged for parts and labor by all other franchised motor vehicle dealers in the dealer's market offering the same line-make vehicles. In the event there are no other franchised dealers offering the same line-make of vehicle in the dealer's market, the manufacturer or distributor may compare the dealer's retail rate for parts and labor with the retail rates charged for parts and labor by other franchised dealers who are selling competing line-makes of vehicles within the dealer's market. The retail rate and the average labor rate shall go into effect 30 days following the manufacturer's approval, but in no event later than 60 days following the declaration, subject to audit of the submitted repair orders by the manufacturer or distributor and a rebuttal of the declared rate as described above. If the declared rate is rebutted, the manufacturer or distributor shall propose an adjustment of the average percentage markup based on that rebuttal not later than 30 days after such audit, but in no event later than 60 days after submission. If the dealer does not agree with the proposed average percentage markup, the dealer may file a protest with the Commissioner not later than 30 days after receipt of that proposal by the manufacturer or distributor. If such a protest is filed, the Commissioner shall inform the manufacturer or distributor that a timely protest has been filed and that a hearing will be held on such protest. In any hearing held pursuant to this subsection, the manufacturer or distributor shall have the burden of proving by a preponderance of the evidence that the rate declared by the dealer was unreasonable as described in this subsection and that the proposed adjustment of the average percentage markup is reasonable pursuant to the provisions of this subsection. If the dealer prevails at a protest hearing, the dealer's proposed rate, affirmed at the hearing, shall be effective as of 60 days after the date of the dealer's initial submission of the customer-paid service orders to the manufacturer or distributor. If the manufacturer or distributor prevails at a protest hearing, the rate proposed by the manufacturer or distributor, that was affirmed at the hearing, shall be effective beginning 30 days following issuance of the final order.

(a2)   In calculating the retail rate customarily charged by the dealer for parts and labor, the following work shall not be included in the calculation:

(1)   Repairs for manufacturer or distributor special events, specials, or promotional discounts for retail customer repairs.

(2)   Parts sold at wholesale or at reduced or specially negotiated rates for insurance repairs.

(3)   Engine assemblies.

(4)   Routine maintenance not covered under warranty, such as fluids, filters, and belts not provided in the course of repairs.

(5)   Nuts, bolts, fasteners, and similar items that do not have an individual part number.

(6)   Tires.

(7) Vehicle reconditioning.

(8) Batteries and light bulbs.

(a3) If a manufacturer or distributor furnishes a part or component to a dealer, at no cost, to use in performing repairs under a recall, campaign service action, or warranty repair, the manufacturer or distributor shall compensate the dealer for the part or component in the same manner as warranty parts compensation under this section by compensating the dealer the average markup on the cost for the part or component as listed in the manufacturer's or distributor's price schedule less the cost for the part or component.

(a4) A manufacturer or distributor may not require a dealer to establish the retail rate customarily charged by the dealer for parts and labor by an unduly burdensome or time-consuming method or by requiring information that is unduly burdensome or time consuming to provide, including, but not limited to, part-by-part or transaction-by-transaction calculations.

(b) Notwithstanding the terms of any franchise agreement, it is unlawful for any motor vehicle manufacturer, factory branch, distributor, or distributor branch to fail to perform any of its warranty obligations with respect to a motor vehicle, to fail to fully compensate its motor vehicle dealers licensed in this State for warranty parts other than parts used to repair the living facilities of recreational vehicles, at the prevailing retail rate according to the factors in subsection (a) of this section, or, in service in accordance with the schedule of compensation provided the dealer pursuant to subsection (a) above, or to otherwise recover all or any portion of its costs for compensating its motor vehicle dealers licensed in this State for warranty parts and service either by reduction in the amount due to the dealer, or by separate charge, surcharge, or other imposition, and to fail to indemnify and hold harmless its franchised dealers licensed in this State against any judgment for damages or settlements agreed to by the manufacturer, including, but not limited to, court costs and reasonable attorneys' fees of the motor vehicle dealer, arising out of complaints, claims or lawsuits including, but not limited to, strict liability, negligence, misrepresentation, express or implied warranty, or recision or revocation of acceptance of the sale of a motor vehicle as defined in G.S. 25-2-608, to the extent that the judgment or settlement relates to the alleged defective negligent manufacture, assembly or design of new motor vehicles, parts or accessories or other functions by the manufacturer, factory branch, distributor or distributor branch, beyond the control of the dealer. Any audit for warranty parts or service compensation shall only be for the 12-month period immediately following the date of the payment of the claim by the manufacturer, factory branch, distributor, or distributor branch. Any audit for sales incentives, service incentives, rebates, or other forms of incentive compensation shall only be for the 12-month period immediately following the date of the payment of the claim by the manufacturer, factory branch, distributor, or distributor branch pursuant to a sales incentives program, service incentives program, rebate program, or other form of incentive compensation program. Provided, however, these limitations shall not be effective in the case of fraudulent claims.

(b1)   All claims made by motor vehicle dealers pursuant to this section for compensation for delivery, preparation, warranty and recall work including labor, parts, and other expenses, shall be paid by the manufacturer within 30 days after receipt of claim from the dealer. When any claim is disapproved, the dealer shall be notified in writing of the grounds for disapproval. Any claim not specifically disapproved in writing within 30 days after receipt shall be considered approved and payment is due immediately. No claim which has been approved and paid may be charged back to the dealer unless it can be shown that the claim was false or fraudulent, that the repairs were not properly made or were unnecessary to correct the defective condition, or the dealer failed to reasonably substantiate the claim either in accordance with the manufacturer's reasonable written procedures or by other reasonable means. A manufacturer or distributor shall not deny a claim or reduce the amount to be reimbursed to the dealer as long as the dealer has provided reasonably sufficient documentation that the dealer:

(1)   Made a good faith attempt to perform the work in compliance with the written policies and procedures of the manufacturer; and

(2)   Actually performed the work.

Notwithstanding the foregoing, a manufacturer shall not fail to fully compensate a dealer for warranty or recall work or make any chargeback to the dealer's account based on the dealer's failure to comply with the manufacturer's claim documentation procedure or procedures unless both of the following requirements have been met:

(1)   The dealer has, within the previous 12 months, failed to comply with the same specific claim documentation procedure or procedures; and

(2)   The manufacturer has, within the previous 12 months, provided a written warning to the dealer by certified United States mail, return receipt requested,

identifying the specific claim documentation procedure or procedures violated by the dealer.

Nothing contained in this subdivision shall be deemed to prevent or prohibit a manufacturer from adopting or implementing a policy or procedure which provides or allows for the self-audit of dealers, provided, however, that if any such self-audit procedure contains provisions relating to claim documentation, such claim documentation policies or procedures shall be subject to the prohibitions and requirements contained in this subdivision. Notices sent by a manufacturer under a bona fide self-audit procedure shall be deemed sufficient notice to meet the requirements of this subsection provided that the dealer is given reasonable opportunity through self-audit to identify and correct any out-of-line procedures for a period of at least 60 days before the manufacturer conducts its own audit of the dealer warranty operations and procedures. A manufacturer may further not charge a dealer back subsequent to the payment of the claim unless a representative of the manufacturer has met in person at the dealership, or by telephone, with an officer or employee of the dealer designated by the dealer and explained in detail the basis for each of the proposed charge-backs and thereafter given the dealer's representative a reasonable opportunity at the meeting, or during the telephone call, to explain the dealer's position relating to each of the proposed charge-backs. In the event the dealer was selected for audit or review on the basis that some or all of the dealer's claims were viewed as excessive in comparison to average, mean, or aggregate data accumulated by the manufacturer, or in relation to claims submitted by a group of other franchisees of the manufacturer, the manufacturer shall, at or prior to the meeting or telephone call with the dealer's representative, provide the dealer with a written statement containing the basis or methodology upon which the dealer was selected for audit or review.

(b2)   A manufacturer may not deny a motor vehicle dealer's claim for sales incentives, service incentives, rebates, or other forms of incentive compensation, reduce the amount to be paid to the dealer, or charge a dealer back subsequent to the payment of the claim unless it can be shown that the claim was false or fraudulent or that the dealer failed to reasonably substantiate the claim either in accordance with the manufacturer's reasonable written procedures or by other reasonable means.

(b3)   Notwithstanding the terms of any franchise or other agreement, or the terms of any program, policy, or procedure of any manufacturer, it shall be unlawful for a manufacturer to take or threaten to take any adverse action against a dealer located in this State, or to otherwise discriminate against any dealer located in this State, on the basis that the dealer sold or leased a motor vehicle to a customer who either exported the vehicle to a foreign country or who resold the vehicle to a third party, unless the dealer knew or reasonably should have known that the customer intended to export or resell the motor vehicle prior to the customer's purchase of the vehicle from the dealer. The conduct prohibited under this subsection includes, but is not limited to, a manufacturer's actual or threatened: (i) failure or refusal to allocate, sell, or deliver motor vehicles to the dealer; or (ii) discrimination against any dealer in the allocation of vehicles; or (iii) charging back or withholding payments or other compensation or consideration for which a dealer is otherwise eligible for warranty reimbursement or under a sales promotion, incentive program, or contest; or (iv) disqualification of a dealer from participating in or discrimination against any dealer relating to any sales promotion, incentive program, or contest; or (v) termination of a franchise. In any proceeding brought pursuant to this subsection, there shall be a rebuttable presumption that the dealer, prior to the customer's purchase of the vehicle, did not know nor should have reasonably known that the customer intended to export or resell the motor vehicle, if (i) following the sale, the vehicle is titled, registered, and, where applicable, taxes paid in any state or territory within the United States in the name of a customer who was physically present at the dealership at or prior to the time of sale, and (ii) the dealer did not know, prior to the consummation of the sale, that the vehicle would be shipped to a foreign country.

(c) In the event there is a dispute between the manufacturer, factory branch, distributor, or distributor branch, and the dealer with respect to any matter referred to in subsection (a), (b), (b1), (b2), or (d) of this section, either party may petition the Commissioner in writing, within 30 days after either party has given written notice of the dispute to the other, for a hearing on the subject and the decision of the Commissioner shall be binding on the parties, subject to rights of judicial review and appeal as provided in Chapter 150B of the General Statutes; provided, however, that nothing contained herein shall give the Commissioner any authority as to the content of any manufacturer's or distributor's warranty. Upon the filing of a petition before the Commissioner under this subsection, any chargeback to or any payment required of a dealer by a manufacturer relating to warranty parts or service compensation, or to sales incentives, service incentives, rebates, or other forms of incentive compensation, shall be stayed during the pendency of the determination by the Commissioner.

(d) Transportation damages. -

(1) Notwithstanding the terms, provisions or conditions of any agreement or franchise, the manufacturer is liable for all damages to motor vehicles before delivery to a carrier or transporter.

(2) If a new motor vehicle dealer determines the method of transportation, the risk of loss passes to the dealer upon delivery of the vehicle to the carrier.

(3) In every other instance, the risk of loss remains with the manufacturer until such time as the new motor vehicle dealer or his designee accepts the vehicle from the carrier.

(4) Whenever a motor vehicle is damaged while in transit when the carrier or the means of transportation is designated by the manufacturer or distributor, or whenever a motor vehicle is otherwise damaged prior to delivery to the dealer, the dealer must:

a. Notify the manufacturer or distributor of such damage within three working days or within such additional time as authorized by the franchise agreement of the occurrence of the delivery of the motor vehicle as defined in subsection (1) of this section; and

b. Must request from the manufacturer or distributor authorization to repair the damages sustained or to replace the parts or accessories damaged.

(5) In the event the manufacturer or distributor refuses or fails to authorize repair or replacement of any such damage within ten working days after receipt of notification of damage by the dealer, ownership of the motor vehicle shall revert to the manufacturer or distributor, and the dealer shall incur no obligation, financial or otherwise, for such damage to the motor vehicle.

(5a) No manufacturer shall fail to disclose in writing to a new motor vehicle dealer, at the time of delivery of a new motor vehicle, the nature and extent of any and all damage and post-manufacturing repairs made to such motor vehicle while in the possession or under the control of the manufacturer if the cost of such post-manufacturing repairs exceeds three percent (3%) of the manufacturer's suggested retail price. A manufacturer is not required to disclose to a new motor vehicle dealer that any glass, tires or bumper of a new motor vehicle was damaged at any time if the damaged item has been replaced with original or comparable equipment.

(6) Nothing in this subsection (d) shall relieve the dealer of the obligation to cooperate with the manufacturer as necessary in filing any transportation damage claim with the carrier.

(e) Damage/Repair Disclosure. - Notwithstanding the provisions of subdivision (d)(4) of this section and in supplementation thereof, a new motor vehicle dealer shall disclose in writing to a purchaser of the new motor vehicle prior to entering into a sales contract any damage and repair to the new motor vehicle if the damage exceeds five percent (5%) of the manufacturer's suggested retail price as calculated at the rate of the dealer's authorized warranty rate for labor and parts.

(1) A new motor vehicle dealer is not required to disclose to a purchaser that any damage of any nature occurred to a new motor vehicle at any time if the total cost of all repairs fails to exceed five percent (5%) of the manufacturer's suggested retail price as calculated at the time the repairs were made based upon the dealer's authorized warranty rate for labor and parts and the damaged item has been replaced with original or comparable equipment.

(2) If disclosure is not required under this section, a purchaser may not revoke or rescind a sales contract or have or file any cause of action or claim against the dealer or manufacturer for breach of contract, breach of warranty, fraud, concealment, unfair and deceptive acts or practices, or otherwise due solely to the fact that the new motor vehicle was damaged and repaired prior to completion of the sale.

(3) For purposes of this section, "manufacturer's suggested retail price" means the retail price of the new motor vehicle suggested by the manufacturer including the retail delivered price suggested by the manufacturer for each accessory or item of optional equipment physically attached to the new motor vehicle at the time of delivery to the new motor vehicle dealer which is not included within the retail price suggested by the manufacturer for the new motor vehicle.

(f) The provisions of subsections (a), (b), (b1), (d) and (e) shall not apply to manufacturers and dealers of "motorcycles" as defined in G.S. 20-4.01(27).

(f1) The provisions of subsections (a), (b), (b1), (b2), and (c) of this section applicable to a motor vehicle manufacturer shall also apply to a component parts manufacturer. For purposes of this section, a component parts manufacturer means a person, resident, or nonresident of this State who manufactures or assembles new motor vehicle "component parts" and directly warrants the component parts to the consumer. For purposes of this section, component parts means an engine, power train, rear axle, or other part of a motor vehicle that is not warranted by the final manufacturer of the motor vehicle.

(f2) The provisions of subsections (d) and (e) of this section shall not apply to a State agency that assists the United States Department of Defense with purchasing, transferring, or titling a vehicle to another State agency, a unit of local government, a volunteer fire department, or a volunteer rescue squad.

(g) Truck Dealer Cost Reimbursement. - Every manufacturer, manufacturer branch, distributor, or distributor branch of new motor vehicles, or any affiliate or subsidiary thereof, which manufactures or distributes new motor vehicles with a gross vehicle weight rating of 16,000 pounds or more shall compensate its new motor vehicle dealers located in this State for the cost of special tools, equipment, and training for which its dealers are liable when the applicable manufacturer, manufacturer branch, distributor, or distributor branch sells a portion of its vehicle inventory to converters and other nondealer retailers. The purpose of this reimbursement is to compensate truck dealers for special additional costs these dealers are required to pay for servicing these vehicles when the dealers are excluded from compensation for these expenses at the point of sale. The compensation which shall be paid pursuant to this subsection shall be applicable only with respect to new motor vehicles with a gross vehicle weight rating of 16,000 pounds or more which are registered to end users within this State and that are sold by a manufacturer, manufacturer branch, distributor, or distributor branch to either:

(1) Persons or entities other than new motor vehicle dealers with whom the manufacturer, manufacturer branch, distributor, or distributor branch has entered into franchises; or

(2) Persons or entities that install custom bodies on truck chassis, including, but not limited to, mounted equipment or specialized bodies for concrete distribution, firefighting equipment, waste disposal, recycling, garbage disposal, buses, utility service, street sweepers, wreckers, and rollback bodies for vehicle recovery; provided, however, that no compensation shall be required to be paid pursuant to this subdivision with respect to vehicles sold for purposes of manufacturing or assembling school buses.

The amount of compensation which shall be payable by the applicable manufacturer, manufacturer branch, distributor, or distributor branch shall be six hundred dollars ($600.00) per new motor vehicle registered in this State whose chassis has a gross vehicle weight rating of 16,000 pounds or more. The compensation required pursuant to this subsection shall be paid by the applicable manufacturer, manufacturer branch, distributor, or distributor branch to its franchised new motor vehicle dealer in closest proximity to the registered address of the end user to whom the motor vehicle has been registered within 30 days after such registration. Upon receiving a request in writing from one of its franchised dealers located in this State, a manufacturer, manufacturer branch, distributor, or distributor branch shall promptly make available to such dealer its records relating to the registered addresses of its new motor vehicles registered in this State for the previous 12 months and its payment of compensation to dealers as provided in this subsection.

(h) Notwithstanding the terms of any franchise agreement, it is unlawful for any motor vehicle manufacturer, factory branch, distributor, or distributor branch to deny a franchised new motor vehicle dealer the right to return any part or accessory that the dealer has not sold after 15 months where the part or accessory was not obtained through a specific order initiated by the franchised new motor vehicle dealer but instead was specified for, sold to, and shipped to the dealer pursuant to an automated ordering system, provided that such part or accessory is in the condition required for return to the manufacturer, factory branch, distributor, or distributor branch and the dealer returns the part within 60 days of it becoming eligible under this subsection. For purposes of this subsection, an "automated ordering system" shall be a computerized system required by the manufacturer that automatically specifies parts and accessories for sale and shipment to the dealer without specific order thereof initiated by the dealer. The manufacturer, factory branch, distributor, or distributor branch shall not charge a restocking or handling fee for any part or accessory being returned under this subsection. (1973, c. 88, s. 3; c. 1331, s. 3; 1983, c. 704, ss. 11-13; 1987, c. 827, s. 1; 1989, c. 614, ss. 1, 2; 1991, c. 561, ss. 1-4; 1993, c. 116, ss. 1, 2; 1995, c. 156, s. 1; 1997-319, s. 4; 1999-335, ss. 3, 3.1, 4; 2003-113, s. 5; 2003-258, s. 4; 2007-513, ss. 5-7, 11; 2009-338, ss. 3, 4; 2009-550, s. 2(c); 2011-290, s. 10; 2013-302, s. 10.)

§ 20-305.2. Unfair methods of competition.

(a) It is unlawful for any motor vehicle manufacturer, factory branch, distributor, distributor branch, or subsidiary thereof, to directly or indirectly through any subsidiary or affiliated entity, own any ownership interest in, operate, or control any motor vehicle dealership in this State, provided that this section shall not be construed to prohibit:

(1)   The operation by a manufacturer, factory branch, distributor, distributor branch, or subsidiary thereof, of a dealership for a temporary period (not to exceed one year) during the transition from one owner or operator to another; or

(2)   The ownership or control of a dealership by a manufacturer, factory branch, distributor, distributor branch, or subsidiary thereof, while in a bona fide relationship with an economically disadvantaged or other independent person, other than a manufacturer, factory branch, distributor, distributor branch, or an agent or affiliate thereof, who has made a bona fide, unencumbered initial investment of at least six percent (6%) of the total sales price that is subject to loss in the dealership and who can reasonably expect to acquire full ownership of the dealership within a reasonable period of time, not to exceed 12 years, and on reasonable terms and conditions; or

(3)   The ownership, operation or control of a dealership by a manufacturer, factory branch, distributor, distributor branch, or subsidiary thereof, if such manufacturer, factory branch, distributor, distributor branch, or subsidiary has been engaged in the retail sale of motor vehicles through such dealership for a continuous period of three years prior to March 16, 1973, and if the Commissioner determines, after a hearing on the matter at the request of any party, that there is no independent dealer available in the relevant market area to own and operate the franchise in a manner consistent with the public interest; or

(4)   The ownership, operation, or control of a dealership by a manufacturer, factory branch, distributor, distributor branch, or subsidiary thereof, if the Commissioner determines after a hearing on the matter at the request of any party, that there is no independent dealer available in the relevant market area to own and operate the franchise in a manner consistent with the public interest; or

(5)   The ownership, operation, or control of any facility (location) of a new motor vehicle dealer in this State at which the dealer sells only new and used motor vehicles with a gross weight rating of 8,500 pounds or more, provided that both of the following conditions have been met:

a.   The facility is located within 35 miles of manufacturing or assembling facilities existing as of January 1, 1999, and is owned or operated by the manufacturer, manufacturing branch, distributor, distributor branch, or any affiliate or subsidiary thereof which assembles, manufactures, or distributes new motor vehicles with a gross weight rating of 8,500 pounds or more by such dealer at said location; and

b. The facility is located in the largest Standard Metropolitan Statistical Area (SMSA) in the State; or

(6) As to any line make of motor vehicle for which there is in aggregate no more than 13 franchised new motor vehicle dealers (locations) licensed and in operation within the State as of January 1, 1999, the ownership, operation, or control of one or more new motor vehicle dealership trading solely in such line make of vehicle by the manufacturer, factory branch, distributor, distributor branch, or subsidiary or affiliate thereof, provided however, that all of the following conditions are met:

a. The manufacturer, factory branch, distributor, distributor branch, or subsidiary or affiliate thereof does not own directly or indirectly, in aggregate, in excess of forty-five percent (45%) interest in the dealership;

b. At the time the manufacturer, factory branch, distributor, distributor branch, or subsidiary or affiliate thereof first acquires ownership or assumes operation or control with respect to any such dealership, the distance between the dealership thus owned, operated, or controlled and the nearest other new motor vehicle dealership trading in the same line make of vehicle, is no less than 35 miles;

c. All the manufacturer's franchise agreements confer rights on the dealer of the line make to develop and operate within a defined geographic territory or area, as many dealership facilities as the dealer and manufacturer shall agree are appropriate; and

d. That as of July 1, 1999, not fewer than half of the dealers of the line make within the State own and operate two or more dealership facilities in the geographic territory or area covered by the franchise agreement with the manufacturer.

(7) The ownership, operation, or control of a dealership that sells primarily recreational vehicles as defined in G.S. 20-4.01 by a manufacturer, factory branch, distributor, or distributor branch, or subsidiary thereof, if the

manufacturer, factory branch, distributor, or distributor branch, or subsidiary thereof, owned, operated, or controlled the dealership as of October 1, 2001.

(b)   Subsection (a) of this section does not apply to manufacturers or distributors of trailers or semitrailers that are not recreational vehicles as defined in G.S. 20-4.01.

(c)   For purposes of subsection (d) of this section, the following definitions apply:

(1)   Former Franchisee. - A new motor vehicle dealer, as defined in G.S. 20-286(13), that has entered into a franchise, as defined in G.S. 20-286(8a) with a predecessor manufacturer and that has either:

a.   Entered into a termination agreement or deferred termination agreement with a predecessor or successor manufacturer related to such franchise; or

b.   Has had such franchise canceled, terminated, nonrenewed, noncontinued, rejected, nonassumed, or otherwise ended.

(2)   Relevant market area. - The area within a 10-, 15-, or 20-mile radius around the site of the previous franchisee's dealership facility, as determined in the same manner that the relevant market area is determined under G.S. 20-286(13b) when a manufacturer is seeking to establish an additional new motor vehicle dealer.

(3)   Successor manufacturer. - Any motor vehicle manufacturer, as defined in G.S. 20-286(8e), that, on or after January 1, 2009, acquires, succeeds to, or assumes any part of the business of another manufacturer, referred to as the "predecessor manufacturer," as the result of any of the following:

a.   A change in ownership, operation, or control of the predecessor manufacturer by sale or transfer of assets, corporate stock or other equity interest, assignment, merger, consolidation, combination, joint venture, redemption, court-approved sale, operation of law or otherwise.

b.   The termination, suspension, or cessation of a part or all of the business operations of the predecessor manufacturer.

c.   The discontinuance of the sale of the product line.

d. A change in distribution system by the predecessor manufacturer, whether through a change in distributor or the predecessor manufacturer's decision to cease conducting business through a distributor altogether.

(d) For a period of four years from the date that a successor manufacturer acquires, succeeds to, or assumes any part of the business of a predecessor manufacturer, it shall be unlawful for such successor manufacturer to enter into a same line make franchise with any person, as defined in G.S. 20-4.01(28), or to permit the relocation of any existing same line make franchise, for a line make of the predecessor manufacturer that would be located or relocated within the relevant market area of a former franchisee who owned or leased a dealership facility in that relevant market area without first offering the additional or relocated franchise to the former franchisee, or the designated successor of such former franchisee in the event the former franchisee is deceased or disabled, at no cost and without any requirements or restrictions other than those imposed generally on the manufacturer's other franchisees at that time, unless one of the following applies:

(1) As a result of the former franchisee's cancellation, termination, noncontinuance, or nonrenewal of the franchise, the predecessor manufacturer had consolidated the line make with another of its line makes for which the predecessor manufacturer had a franchisee with a then-existing dealership facility located within that relevant market area.

(2) The successor manufacturer has paid the former franchisee, or the designated successor of such former franchisee in the event the former franchisee is deceased or disabled, the fair market value of the former franchisee's franchise calculated as prescribed in G.S. 20-305(6)d.3.

(3) The successor manufacturer proves that the former franchisee, or the designated successor of such former franchisee in the event the former franchisee is deceased or disabled, by reason of lack of training, lack of prior experience, poor past performance, lack of financial ability, or poor character, is unfit to own or manage the dealership. A successor manufacturer who seeks to assert that a former franchisee is unfit to own or manage the dealership must file a petition seeking a hearing on this issue before the Commissioner and shall have the burden of proving lack of fitness at such hearing. The Commissioner shall try to conduct the hearing and render a final determination within 120 days after the manufacturer's petition has been filed. No successor dealer, other than the former franchisee, may be appointed or franchised by the successor manufacturer within the relevant market area until the Commissioner has held a

hearing and rendered a determination on the issue of the fitness of the previous franchisee to own or manage the dealership.

(e)   For purposes of this section, an unfair method of competition includes any physical or mechanical warranty repair made or provided directly by a manufacturer or distributor to any motor vehicle located within this State requiring the direct participation of a dealer franchised by the manufacturer or distributor and without such dealer receiving reasonable compensation, equal to an amount no less than the amount provided in G.S. 20-305.1.

(f)   No claim or cause of action may be brought against a dealer in this State arising out of any warranty repair, fix, repair, or update that was provided by the manufacturer or distributor without the direct involvement and participation of the dealer. Any manufacturer or distributor that provides or attempts to provide a warranty repair, fix, repair, update, or adjustment directly to any motor vehicle located within this State without the direct participation of a dealer franchised by the manufacturer or distributor shall fully indemnify and hold harmless any dealer located in this State for all claims, demands, judgments, damages, attorneys' fees, litigation expenses, and all other costs and expenses incurred by the dealer arising out of the actual or attempted warranty repair, fix, repair, update, or adjustment. (1973, c. 88, s. 3; 1983, c. 704, ss. 14, 15; 1999-335, s. 5; 2001-510, s. 3; 2002-72, ss. 19(d), 19(e); 2003-416, s. 11; 2009-496, s. 2; 2013-302, s. 8.)

§ 20-305.3. Hearing notice.

In every case of a hearing before the Commissioner authorized under this Article, the Commissioner shall give reasonable notice of each such hearing to all interested parties, and the Commissioner's decision shall be binding on the parties, subject to the rights of judicial review and appeal as provided in Chapter 150B of the General Statutes. The costs of such hearings shall be assessed by the Commissioner. (1973, c. 88, s. 3; c. 1331, s. 3; 1987, c. 827, s. 1.)

§ 20-305.4. Motor Vehicle Dealers' Advisory Board.

(a)   The Motor Vehicle Dealers' Advisory Board shall consist of six members; three of which shall be appointed by the Speaker of the House of

Representatives, and three of which shall be appointed by the President Pro Tempore of the Senate to consult with and advise the Commissioner with respect to matters brought before the Commissioner under the provisions of G.S. 20-304 through 20-305.4.

(b) Each member of the Motor Vehicle Dealers' Advisory Board shall be a resident of North Carolina. Three members of the Board shall be franchised dealers in new automobiles or trucks, duly licensed and engaged in business as such in North Carolina, provided that no two of such dealers may be franchised to sell automobiles or trucks manufactured or distributed by the same person or a subsidiary or affiliate of the same person. Three members of the Board shall not be motor vehicle dealers or employees of a motor vehicle dealer.

(c) The Speaker shall appoint two of the dealer members and one of the public members and shall fill any vacancy in said positions and the President Pro Tempore of the Senate shall appoint one of the dealer members and two of the public members and shall fill any vacancy in said positions. In making the initial appointments the Speaker shall designate that the two dealer members shall serve for one and three years respectively and the public member shall serve for two years, and in making the initial appointments the Lieutenant Governor shall designate that the dealer member shall serve for two years and the two public members shall serve for one and three years respectively.

(d) Two members of the first Board appointed shall serve for a period of three years, two members of the first Board shall serve for a period of two years, and two members of the first Board shall serve for a period of one year. Subsequent appointments shall be for terms of three years, except appointments to fill vacancies which shall be for the unexpired terms. Members of the Board shall meet at the call of the Commissioner and shall receive as compensation for their services seven dollars ($7.00) for each day actually engaged in the exercise of the duties of the Board and such travel expenses and subsistence allowances as are generally allowed other State commissions and boards. (1973, c. 88, s. 3; 1995, c. 490, s. 36.)

§ 20-305.5. Sections 20-305, subdivisions (4) through (28), and 20-305.1 to 20-305.4 not applicable to certain manufacturers and dealers.

The provisions of G.S. 20-305(4) through G.S. 20-305(28) and 20-305.1 to 20-305.4 shall not apply to manufacturers of, or dealers in, mobile or manufactured type housing or recreational trailers. (1973, c. 88, s. 4; 1983, c. 704, s. 18.)

§ 20-305.6. Unlawful for manufacturers to unfairly discriminate among dealers.

Notwithstanding the terms of any contract, franchise, novation, or agreement, it shall be unlawful for any manufacturer, factory branch, distributor, or distributor branch to do any of the following:

(1)   Discriminate against any similarly situated franchised new motor vehicle dealers in this State.

(2)   Unfairly discriminate against franchised new motor vehicle dealers located in this State who have dualed facilities at which the vehicles distributed by the manufacturer, factory branch, distributor, or distributor branch are sold or serviced with one or more other line makes of vehicles.

(3)   Unfairly discriminate against one of its franchised new motor vehicle dealers in this State with respect to any aspect of the franchise agreement.

(4)   Use any financial services company or leasing company owned or controlled by the manufacturer or distributor to accomplish what would otherwise be illegal conduct on the part of the manufacturer or distributor pursuant to this section. This section shall not limit the right of the financial services or leasing company to engage in business practices in accordance with the trade. (2001-510, s. 4.)

§ 20-305.7. Protecting dealership data and consent to access dealership information.

(a)   Except as expressly authorized in this section, no manufacturer, factory branch, distributor, or distributor branch shall require a new motor vehicle dealer to provide its customer lists, customer information, consumer contact information, transaction data, or service files. Any requirement by a manufacturer, factory branch, distributor, or distributor branch that a new motor vehicle dealer provide its customer lists, customer information, consumer contact information, transaction data, or service files as a condition to the dealer's participation in any incentive program or contest for a customer or dealer to receive any incentive payments otherwise earned under an incentive program or contest, for the dealer to obtain consumer or customer leads, or for the dealer to receive any other benefits, rights, merchandise, or services for which the dealer would otherwise be entitled to obtain under the franchise or any other contract or agreement, or which shall customarily be provided to dealers, shall be voidable at the option of the dealer, unless all of the following conditions are satisfied: (i) the customer information requested relates solely to the specific program requirements or goals associated with such manufacturer's or distributor's own vehicle makes and does not require that the dealer provide general customer information or other information related to the dealer; (ii) such requirement is lawful and would also not require the dealer to allow any customer the right to opt out under the federal Gramm-Leach-Bliley Act, 15 U.S.C., Subchapter I, § 1608, et seq.; and (iii) the dealer is not required to allow the manufacturer or distributor or any third party to have direct access to the dealer's computer system, but the dealer is instead permitted to provide the same dealer, consumer, or customer data or information specified by the manufacturer or distributor by timely obtaining and pushing or otherwise furnishing the required data in a widely accepted file format such as comma delimited in accordance with subsection (g1) of this section. Nothing contained in this section shall limit the ability of the manufacturer, factory branch, distributor, or distributor branch to require that the dealer provide, or use in accordance with the law, such customer information related solely to such manufacturer's or distributor's own vehicle makes to the extent necessary to do any of the following:

(1) Satisfy any safety or recall notice obligations.

(2) Complete the sale and delivery of a new motor vehicle to a customer.

(3) Validate and pay customer or dealer incentives.

(4) Submit to the manufacturer, factory branch, distributor, or distributor branch claims for any services supplied by the dealer for any claim for warranty parts or repairs.

At the request of a manufacturer or distributor or of a third party acting on behalf of a manufacturer or distributor, a dealer may only be required to provide customer information related solely to such manufacturer's or distributor's own vehicle makes for reasonable marketing purposes, market research, consumer surveys, market analysis, and dealership performance analysis, but the dealer is only required to provide such customer information to the extent lawfully permissible; to the extent the requested information relates solely to specific program requirements or goals associated with such manufacturer's or distributor's own vehicle makes and does not require the dealer to provide general customer information or other information related to the dealer; and to the extent the requested information can be provided without requiring that the dealer allow any customer the right to opt out under the federal Gramm-Leach-Bliley Act, 15 U.S.C., Subchapter I, § 6801, et seq.

No manufacturer, factory branch, distributor, or distributor branch shall access or obtain dealer or customer data from or write dealer or customer data to a dealer management computer system utilized by a motor vehicle dealer located in this State, or require or coerce a motor vehicle dealer located in this State to utilize a particular dealer management computer system, unless the dealer management computer system allows the dealer to reasonably maintain the security, integrity, and confidentiality of the data maintained in the system. No manufacturer, factory branch, distributor, distributor branch, dealer management computer system vendor, or any third party acting on behalf of any manufacturer, factory branch, distributor, distributor branch, or dealer management computer system vendor shall prohibit a dealer from providing a means to regularly and continually monitor the specific data accessed from or written to the dealer's computer system and from complying with applicable State and federal laws and any rules or regulations promulgated thereunder. These provisions shall not be deemed to impose an obligation on a manufacturer, factory branch, distributor, distributor branch, dealer management computer system vendor, or any third party acting on behalf of any manufacturer, factory branch, distributor, distributor branch, or dealer management computer system vendor to provide such capability.

(b) No manufacturer, factory branch, distributor, distributor branch, dealer management computer system vendor, or any third party acting on behalf of any manufacturer, factory branch, distributor, distributor branch, or dealer management computer system vendor may access or utilize customer or prospect information maintained in a dealer management computer system utilized by a motor vehicle dealer located in this State for purposes of soliciting any such customer or prospect on behalf of, or directing such customer or prospect to, any other dealer. The limitations in this subsection do not apply to:

(1) A customer that requests a reference to another dealership;

(2) A customer that moves more than 60 miles away from the dealer whose data was accessed;

(3) Customer or prospect information that was provided to the dealer by the manufacturer, factory branch, distributor, or distributor branch; or

(4) Customer or prospect information obtained by the manufacturer, factory branch, distributor, or distributor branch where the dealer agrees to allow the manufacturer, factory branch, distributor, distributor branch, dealer management computer system vendor, or any third party acting on behalf of any manufacturer, factory branch, distributor, distributor branch, or dealer management computer system vendor the right to access and utilize the customer or prospect information maintained in the dealer's dealer management computer system for purposes of soliciting any customer or prospect of the dealer on behalf of, or directing such customer or prospect to, any other dealer in a separate, stand-alone written instrument dedicated solely to such authorization.

No manufacturer, factory branch, distributor, distributor branch, dealer management computer system vendor, or any third party acting on behalf of any manufacturer, factory branch, distributor, distributor branch, or dealer management computer system vendor, may provide access to customer or dealership information maintained in a dealer management computer system utilized by a motor vehicle dealer located in this State, without first obtaining the dealer's prior express written consent, revocable by the dealer upon five business days written notice, to provide such access. Prior to obtaining said consent and prior to entering into an initial contract or renewal of a contract with a dealer located in this State, the manufacturer, factory branch, distributor, distributor branch, dealer management computer system vendor, or any third party acting on behalf of, or through any manufacturer, factory branch, distributor, distributor branch, or dealer management computer system vendor shall provide to the dealer a written list of all specific third parties to whom any data obtained from the dealer has actually been provided within the 12-month period ending November 1 of the prior year. The list shall further describe the scope and specific fields of the data provided. In addition to the initial list, a dealer management computer system vendor or any third party acting on behalf of, or through a dealer management computer system vendor shall provide to the dealer an annual list of third parties to whom said data is actually being provided on November 1 of each year and to whom said data has actually been provided in the preceding 12 months and describe the scope and specific fields of the data provided. Such list shall be provided to the dealer by January 1 of each year. Any dealer management computer system vendor's contract that directly relates to the transfer or accessing of dealer or dealer customer information must conspicuously state, "NOTICE TO DEALER: THIS AGREEMENT RELATES TO THE TRANSFER AND ACCESSING OF CONFIDENTIAL INFORMATION AND CONSUMER RELATED DATA". Such consent does not change any such person's obligations to comply with the terms of this section and any additional State or federal laws (and any rules or regulations promulgated thereunder) applicable to them with respect to such access. In addition, no dealer management computer system vendor may refuse to provide a dealer management computer system to a motor vehicle dealer located in this State if the dealer refuses to provide any consent under this subsection.

(c)   No dealer management computer system vendor, or third party acting on behalf of or through any dealer management computer system vendor, may access or obtain data from or write data to a dealer management computer system utilized by a motor vehicle dealer located in this State, unless the dealer management computer system allows the dealer to reasonably maintain the security, integrity, and confidentiality of the customer and dealership information maintained in the system. No dealer management computer system vendor, or third party acting on behalf of or through any dealer management computer system vendor, shall prohibit a dealer from providing a means to regularly and continually monitor the specific data accessed from or written to the dealer's computer system and from complying with applicable State and federal laws and any rules or regulations promulgated thereunder. These provisions shall not be deemed to impose an obligation on a manufacturer, factory branch, distributor, distributor branch, dealer management computer system vendor, or any third party acting on behalf of any manufacturer, factory branch, distributor, distributor branch, or dealer management computer system vendor to provide such capability.

(d)   Any manufacturer, factory branch, distributor, distributor branch, dealer management computer system vendor, or any third party acting on behalf of or through any dealer management computer system vendor, having electronic access to customer or motor vehicle dealership data in a dealership management computer system utilized by a motor vehicle dealer located in this State shall provide notice to the dealer of any security breach of dealership or customer data obtained through such access, which at the time of the breach was in the possession or custody of the manufacturer, factory branch, distributor, distributor branch, dealer management computer system vendor, or third party. The disclosure notification shall be made without unreasonable delay by the manufacturer, factory branch, distributor, distributor branch, dealer management computer system vendor, or third party following discovery by the person, or notification to the person, of the breach. The disclosure notification shall describe measures reasonably necessary to determine the scope of the breach and corrective actions which may be taken in an effort to restore the integrity, security, and confidentiality of such data. Such measures and corrective actions shall be implemented as soon as practicable by all persons responsible for the breach.

(e) Nothing in this section shall preclude, prohibit, or deny the right of the manufacturer, factory branch, distributor, or distributor branch to receive customer or dealership information from a motor vehicle dealer located in this State for the purposes of complying with federal or State safety requirements or implementing steps related to manufacturer recalls at such times as necessary in order to comply with federal and State requirements or manufacturer recalls provided that receiving this information from the dealer does not impair, alter, or reduce the security, integrity, and confidentiality of the customer and dealership information collected or generated by the dealer.

(f) The following definitions apply to this section:

(1) "Dealer management computer system" - A computer hardware and software system that is owned or leased by the dealer, including a dealer's use of Web applications, software, or hardware, whether located at the dealership or provided at a remote location and that provides access to customer records and transactions by a motor vehicle dealer located in this State and that allows such motor vehicle dealer timely information in order to sell vehicles, parts or services through such motor vehicle dealership.

(2) "Dealer management computer system vendor" - A seller or reseller of dealer management computer systems, a person that sells computer software for use on dealer management computer systems, or a person who services or maintains dealer management computer systems, but only to the extent that each of the sellers, resellers, or other persons listed in this subdivision are engaged in such activities.

(3) "Security breach" - An incident of unauthorized access to and acquisition of records or data containing dealership or dealership customer information where unauthorized use of the dealership or dealership customer information has occurred or is reasonably likely to occur or that creates a material risk of harm to a dealership or a dealership's customer. Any incident of

unauthorized access to and acquisition of records or data containing dealership or dealership customer information, or any incident of disclosure of dealership customer information to one or more third parties which shall not have been specifically authorized by the dealer or customer, shall constitute a security breach.

(g) The provisions of G.S. 20-308.1(d) shall not apply to an action brought under this section against a dealer management computer system vendor.

(g1) Notwithstanding any of the terms or provisions contained in this section or in any consent, authorization, release, novation, franchise, or other contract or agreement, whenever any manufacturer, factory branch, distributor, distributor branch, dealer management computer system vendor, or any third party acting on behalf of or through, or approved, referred, endorsed, authorized, certified, granted preferred status, or recommended by, any manufacturer, factory branch, distributor, distributor branch, or dealer management computer system vendor requires that a new motor vehicle dealer provide any dealer, consumer, or customer data or information through direct access to a dealer's computer system, the dealer is not required to provide, and may not be required to consent to provide in any written agreement, such direct access to its computer system. The dealer may instead provide the same dealer, consumer, or customer data or information specified by the requesting party by timely obtaining and pushing or otherwise furnishing the requested data to the requesting party in a widely accepted file format such as comma delimited; provided that, when a dealer would otherwise be required to provide direct access to its computer system under the terms of a consent, authorization, release, novation, franchise, or other contract or agreement, a dealer that elects to provide data or information through other means may be charged a reasonable initial set-up fee and a reasonable processing fee based on the actual incremental costs incurred by the party requesting the data for establishing and implementing the process for the dealer. Any term or provision contained in any consent, authorization, release, novation, franchise, or other contract or agreement which is inconsistent with any term or provision contained in this subsection shall be voidable at the option of the dealer.

(g2) Notwithstanding the terms or conditions of any consent, authorization, release, novation, franchise, or other contract or agreement, every manufacturer, factory branch, distributor, distributor branch, dealer management computer system vendor, or any third party acting on behalf of or through any manufacturer, factory branch, distributor, distributor branch, or dealer management computer system vendor, having electronic access to consumer or customer data or other information in a computer system utilized by a new motor vehicle dealer, or who has otherwise been provided consumer or customer data or information by the dealer, shall fully indemnify and hold harmless any dealer from whom it has acquired such consumer or customer data or other information from all damages, costs, and expenses incurred by such dealer. Such indemnification by the manufacturer, factory branch, distributor, distributor branch, dealer management computer system vendor, or third party acting on behalf of these entities includes, but is not limited to, judgments, settlements, fines, penalties, litigation costs, defense costs, court costs, costs related to the disclosure of security breaches, and attorneys' fees arising out of complaints, claims, civil or administrative actions, and, to the fullest extent allowable under the law, governmental investigations and prosecutions to the extent caused by a security breach or the access, storage, maintenance, use, sharing, disclosure, or retention of such dealer's consumer or customer data or other information, or maintenance or services provided to any computer system utilized by a new motor vehicle dealer.

(h) This section shall apply to contracts entered into on or after November 1, 2005. (2005-409, s. 4; 2007-513, s. 10; 2011-290, s. 11; 2013-302, s. 9.)

§ 20-306. Unlawful for salesman to sell except for his employer; multiple employment; persons who arrange transactions involving the sale of new motor vehicles.

It shall be unlawful for any motor vehicle salesman licensed under this Article to sell or exchange or offer or attempt to sell or exchange any motor vehicle other than his own except for the licensed motor vehicle dealer or dealers by whom he is employed, or to offer, transfer or assign, any sale or exchange, that he may have negotiated, to any other dealer or salesman. A salesman may be employed by more than one dealer provided such multiple employment is clearly indicated on his license. It shall be unlawful for any person to, for a fee, commission, or other valuable consideration, arrange or offer to arrange a transaction involving the sale of a new motor vehicle; provided, however, this prohibition shall not be applicable to:

(1) A franchised motor vehicle dealer as defined in G.S. 20-286(8b) who is licensed under this Article or a sales representative who is licensed under this Article when acting on behalf of the dealer;

(2) A manufacturer who is licensed under this Article or bona fide employee of such manufacturer when acting on behalf of the manufacturer;

(3) A distributor who is licensed under this Article or a bona fide employee of such distributor when acting on behalf of the distributor; or

(4) At any point in the transaction the bona fide owner of the vehicle involved in the transaction. (1955, c. 1243, s. 22; 1993, c. 331, s. 3.)

§ 20-307. Article applicable to existing and future franchises and contracts.

The provisions of this Article shall be applicable to all franchises and contracts existing between dealers and manufacturers, factory branches, and distributors at the time of its ratification, and to all such future franchises and contracts. (1955, c. 1243, s. 23.)

§ 20-307.1. Jurisdiction.

A franchisee who is substantially and primarily engaged in the sale of motor vehicles or parts, materials, or components of motor vehicles, including batteries, tires, transmissions, mufflers, painting, lubrication or tune-ups may bring suit against any franchisor, engaged in commerce, in the General Court of Justice in the State of North Carolina that has proper venue. (1983, c. 704, s. 24.)

§ 20-308. Penalties.

Any person violating any of the provisions of this Article, except for G.S. 20-305.7, shall be guilty of a Class 1 misdemeanor. (1955, c. 1243, s. 24; 1993, c. 539, s. 386; 1994, Ex. Sess., c. 24, s. 14(c); 2005-409, s. 5.)

§ 20-308.1. Civil actions for violations.

(a) Notwithstanding the terms, provisions or conditions of any agreement or franchise or other terms or provisions of any novation, waiver or other written instrument, any motor vehicle dealer who is or may be injured by a violation of a provision of this Article, or any party to a franchise who is so injured in his business or property by a violation of a provision of this Article relating to that franchise, or an arrangement which, if consummated, would be in violation of this Article may, notwithstanding the initiation or pendency of, or failure to initiate an administrative proceeding before the Commissioner concerning the same parties or subject matter, bring an action for damages and equitable relief, including injunctive relief, in any court of competent jurisdiction with regard to any matter not within the jurisdiction of the Commissioner or that seeks relief wholly outside the authority or jurisdiction of the Commissioner to award.

(b)   Where the violation of a provision of this Article can be shown to be willful, malicious, or wanton, or if continued multiple violations of a provision or provisions of this Article occur, the court may award punitive damages, attorneys' fees and costs in addition to any other damages under this Article.

(c)   A new motor vehicle dealer, if he has not suffered any loss of money or property, may obtain final equitable relief if it can be shown that the violation of a provision of this Article by a manufacturer or distributor may have the effect of causing a loss of money or property.

(d)   Any association that is comprised of a minimum of 400 new motor vehicle dealers, or a minimum of 10 motorcycle dealers, substantially all of whom are new motor vehicle dealers located within North Carolina, and which represents the collective interests of its members, shall have standing to file a petition before the Commissioner or a cause of action in any court of competent jurisdiction for itself, or on behalf of any or all of its members, seeking declaratory and injunctive relief. Prior to bringing an action, the association and manufacturer, factory branch, distributor, or distributor branch shall initiate mediation as set forth in G.S. 20-301.1(b). An action brought pursuant to this subsection may seek a determination whether one or more manufacturers, factory branches, distributors, or distributor branches doing business in this State have violated any of the provisions of this Article, or for the determination of any rights created or defined by this Article, so long as the association alleges an injury to the collective interest of its members cognizable under this section. A cognizable injury to the collective interest of the members of the association shall be deemed to occur if a manufacturer, factory branch, distributor, or distributor branch doing business in this State has engaged in any conduct or taken any action which actually harms or affects all of the franchised new motor vehicle dealers holding franchises with that manufacturer, factory branch, distributor, or distributor branch in this State. With respect to any administrative or civil action filed by an association pursuant to this subsection, the relief granted shall be limited to declaratory and injunctive relief and in no event shall the Commissioner or court enter an award of monetary damages. (1983, c. 704, s. 16; 1991, c. 510, s. 5; 2001-510, s. 5; 2007-513, s. 8.)

§ 20-308.2. Applicability of this Article.

(a)   Any person who engages directly or indirectly in purposeful contacts within this State in connection with the offering or advertising for sale, or has business dealings, with respect to a new motor vehicle sale within this State, shall be subject to the provisions of this Article and shall be subject to the jurisdiction of the courts of this State.

(b)   The applicability of this Article shall not be affected by a choice of law clause in any franchise, agreement, waiver, novation, or any other written instrument.

(c)   Any provision of any agreement, franchise, waiver, novation or any other written instrument which is in violation of any section of this Article shall be deemed null and void and without force and effect.

(d)   It shall be unlawful for a manufacturer or distributor to use any subsidiary corporation, affiliated corporation, or any other controlled corporation, partnership, association or person to accomplish what would otherwise be illegal conduct under this Article on the part of the manufacturer or distributor.

(e)   The provisions of this Article shall apply to all written agreements between a manufacturer, wholesaler, or distributor with a motor vehicle dealer including, but not limited to, the franchise offering, the franchise agreement, sales of goods, services or advertising, leases or deeds of trust of real or personal property, promises to pay, security interests, pledges, insurance contracts, advertising contracts, construction or installation contracts, servicing contracts, and all other such agreements between a motor vehicle dealer and a manufacturer, wholesaler, or distributor. (1983, c. 704, s. 17; 2005-409, s. 6.)

§§ 20-308.3 through 20-308.12. Reserved for future codification purposes.

Article 12A.

Motor Vehicle Captive Finance Source Law.

§ 20-308.13. Regulation of motor vehicle captive finance sources.

The General Assembly finds and declares that the distribution of motor vehicles in the State of North Carolina vitally affects the general economy of the State and the public interest and public welfare, and in the exercise of its police power, it is necessary to regulate motor vehicle captive finance sources doing business in North Carolina to protect and preserve the investments and properties of the citizens of this State. (2005-409, s. 3.)

§ 20-308.14. Definitions.

The definitions contained in G.S. 20-286 shall be applicable to the provisions of this Article. (2005-409, s. 3.)

§ 20-308.15. Prohibited contractual requirements imposed by manufacturer, distributor, or captive finance source.

It shall be unlawful for any manufacturer, factory branch, captive finance source, distributor, or distributor branch, or any field representative, officer, agent, or any representative of them, notwithstanding the terms, provisions, or conditions of any agreement or franchise, to require any of its franchised dealers located in this State to agree to any terms, conditions, or requirements that are set forth in subdivisions (1) through (8) below in order for any such dealer to sell to any captive finance source (defined below) any retail installment contract, loan, or lease of any motor vehicles purchased or leased by any of the dealer's customers ("contract for sale or lease"), or to be able to participate in, or otherwise, directly or indirectly, obtain the benefits of any consumer transaction incentive program payable to the consumer or the dealer and offered by or through any financial source that provides automotive-related loans or purchases retail installment contracts or lease contracts for motor vehicles in North Carolina and is, directly or indirectly, owned, operated, or controlled by such manufacturer, factory branch, distributor, or distributor branch ("captive finance source"):

(1) Require a dealer to grant such captive finance source a power of attorney to do anything on behalf of the dealer other than sign the dealer's name on any check, draft, or other instrument received in payment or proceeds under any contract for the sale or lease of a motor vehicle that is made payable to the dealer but which is properly payable to the captive finance source, is for the purpose of correcting an error in a customer's finance application or title processing document, or is for the purpose of processing regular titling of the vehicle.

(2) Require a dealer to warrant or guarantee the accuracy and completeness of any personal, financial, or credit information provided by the customer on the credit application and/or in the course of applying for credit other than to require that the dealer make reasonable inquiry regarding the accuracy and completeness of such information and represent that such information is true and correct to the best of the dealer's knowledge.

(3) Require a dealer to repurchase, pay off, or guaranty any contract for the sale or lease of a motor vehicle or to require a dealer to indemnify, defend, or hold harmless the captive finance source for settlements, judgments, damages, litigation expenses, or other costs or expenses incurred by such captive finance source unless the obligation to repurchase, pay off, guaranty, indemnify, or hold harmless resulted directly from (i) the subject dealer's material breach of the terms of a written agreement with the captive finance source or the terms for the purchase of an individual contract for sale or lease that the captive finance source communicates to the dealer before each such purchase, except to the extent the breached terms are otherwise prohibited under subdivisions (1) through (8) of this section, or (ii) the subject dealer's violation of applicable law. For purposes of this section, the dealer may, however, contractually obligate itself to warrant the accuracy of the information provided on the finance contract, but such warranty can only be enforced if the captive finance source gives the dealer a reasonable opportunity to cure or correct any errors on the finance contract where cure or correction is possible. For purposes of this section, any allegation by a third party that would constitute a breach of the terms of a written agreement between the dealer and a captive finance source shall be considered a material breach.

(4) Notwithstanding the terms of any contract or agreement, treat a dealer's breach of an agreement between the dealer and a captive finance source with respect to the captive finance source's purchase of individual contracts for the sale or lease of a motor vehicle as a breach of such agreement with respect to purchase of other such contracts, nor shall such a breach, in and of itself, constitute a breach of any other agreement between the dealer and the captive finance source, or between the dealer and any affiliate of such captive finance source.

(5) Require a dealer to waive any defenses that may be available to it under its agreements with the captive finance source or under any applicable laws.

(6) Require a dealer to settle or contribute any of its own funds or financial resources toward the settlement of any multiparty or class action litigation without obtaining the dealer's voluntary and written consent subsequent to the filing of such litigation.

(7) Require a dealer to contribute to any reserve or contingency account established or maintained by the captive finance source, for the financing of the sale or lease of any motor vehicles purchased or leased by any of the dealer's customers, in any amount or on any basis other than the reasonable expected amount of future finance reserve chargebacks to the dealer's account. This section shall not apply to or limit (i) reasonable amounts reserved and maintained related to the sale or financing of any products ancillary to the sale, lease, or financing of the motor vehicle itself; (ii) a delay or reduction in the payment of dealer's portion of the finance income pursuant to an agreement between the dealer and a captive finance source under which the dealer agrees to such delay or reduction in exchange for the limitation, reduction, or elimination of the dealer's responsibility for finance reserve chargebacks; or (iii) a chargeback to a dealer (or offset of any amounts otherwise payable to a dealer by the captive finance source) for any indebtedness properly owing from a dealer to the captive finance source as part of a specific program covered by this section, the terms of which have been agreed to by the dealer in advance, except to the extent such chargeback would otherwise be prohibited under subdivisions (1) through (8) of this section.

(8) Require a dealer to repossess or otherwise gain possession of a motor vehicle at the request of or on behalf of the captive finance source. This section shall not apply to any requirements contained in any agreement between the dealer and the captive finance source wherein the dealer agrees to receive and

process vehicles that are voluntarily returned by the customer or returned to the lessor at the end of the lease term.

Any clause or provision in any franchise or agreement between a dealer and a manufacturer, factory branch, distributor, or distributor branch, or between a dealer and any captive finance source, that is in violation of or that is inconsistent with any of the provisions of this section shall be voidable, to the extent that it violates this section, at any time at the election of the dealer. (2005-409, s. 3.)

§ 20-308.16. Powers of Commissioner.

(a) The Commissioner shall promote the interests of the retail buyer of motor vehicles.

(b) The Commissioner shall have power to prevent unfair or deceptive acts or practices and other violations of this Article. Any franchised new motor vehicle dealer who believes that a captive finance source with whom the dealer does business in North Carolina has violated or is currently violating any provision of this Article may file a petition before the Commissioner setting forth the factual and legal basis for such violations. The Commissioner shall promptly forward a copy of the petition to the named captive finance source requesting a reply to the petition within 30 days. Allowing for sufficient time for the parties to conduct discovery, the Commissioner or his designee shall then hold an evidentiary hearing and render findings of fact and conclusions of law based on the evidence presented.

(c) The Commissioner shall have the power in hearings arising under this Article to enter scheduling orders and limit the time and scope of discovery; to determine the date, time, and place where hearings are to be held; to subpoena witnesses; to take depositions of witnesses; and to administer oaths.

(d) The Commissioner may, whenever he shall believe from evidence submitted to him that any person has been or is violating any provision of this Article, in addition to any other remedy, bring an action in the name of the State against that person and any other persons concerned or in any way participating in, or about to participate in, practices or acts so in violation, to enjoin any persons from continuing the violations.

(e) The Commissioner may issue rules and regulations to implement the provisions of this section and to establish procedures related to administrative proceedings commenced under this section.

(f) In the event that a dealer, who is permitted or required to file a notice, protest, or petition before the Commissioner within a certain period of time in order to adjudicate, enforce, or protect rights afforded the dealer under this Article, voluntarily elects to appeal a policy, determination, or decision of the captive finance source through an appeals board or internal grievance procedure of the captive finance source, or to participate in or refer the matter to mediation, arbitration, or other alternative dispute resolution procedure or process established or endorsed by the captive finance source, the applicable period of time for the dealer to file the notice, protest, or petition before the Commissioner under this Article shall not commence until the captive finance source's appeal board or internal grievance procedure, mediation, arbitration, or appeals process of the captive finance source has been completed and the dealer has received notice in writing of the final decision or result of the procedure or process. Nothing, however, contained in this subsection shall be deemed to require that any dealer exhaust any internal grievance or other alternative dispute process required or established by the captive finance source before seeking redress from the Commissioner as provided in this Article. (2005-409, s. 3.)

§ 20-308.17. Rules and regulations.

The Commissioner may make such rules and regulations, not inconsistent with the provisions of this Article, as he shall deem necessary or proper for the effective administration and enforcement of this Article, provided that a copy of such rules and regulations shall be mailed to each motor vehicle dealer licensee and captive finance source 30 days prior to the effective date of such rules and regulations. (2005-409, s. 3.)

§ 20-308.18. Hearing notice.

In every case of a hearing before the Commissioner authorized under this Article, the Commissioner shall give reasonable notice of each such hearing to all interested parties, and the Commissioner's decision shall be binding on the parties, subject to the rights of judicial review and appeal as provided in Chapter 150B of the General Statutes. The costs of such hearings shall be assessed by the Commissioner. (2005-409, s. 3.)

§ 20-308.19. Article applicable to existing and future agreements.

The provisions of this Article shall be applicable to all contracts and agreements existing between dealers and captive finance sources at the time of its ratification and to all such future contracts and agreements. (2005-409, s. 3.)

§ 20-308.20. Jurisdiction.

A new motor vehicle dealer located in this State may bring suit against any captive finance source engaged in commerce in this State in the General Court of Justice in the State of North Carolina that has proper venue. (2005-409, s. 3.)

§ 20-308.21. Civil actions for violations.

(a)   Notwithstanding the terms, provisions, or conditions of any agreement or other terms or provisions of any novation, waiver, arbitration agreement, or other written instrument, any person who is or may be injured by a violation of a provision of this Article, or any party to an agreement who is so injured in his business or property by a violation of a provision of this Article relating to that agreement, or an arrangement which, if consummated, would be in violation of this Article may, notwithstanding the initiation or pendency of, or failure to initiate an administrative proceeding before the Commissioner concerning the same parties or subject matter, bring an action for damages and equitable relief, including injunctive relief, in any court of competent jurisdiction with regard to any matter not within the jurisdiction of the Commissioner or that seeks relief wholly outside the authority or jurisdiction of the Commissioner to award.

(b)   Where the violation of a provision of this Article can be shown to be willful, malicious, or wanton, or if continued multiple violations of a provision or provisions of this Article occur, the court may award punitive damages, attorneys' fees and costs in addition to any other damages under this Article.

(c) A new motor vehicle dealer, if he has not suffered any loss of money or property, may obtain final equitable relief if it can be shown that the violation of a provision of this Article by a captive finance source may have the effect of causing a loss of money or property.

(d) Any association that is comprised of a minimum of 400 new motor vehicle dealers, or a minimum of 10 motorcycle dealers, substantially all of whom are new motor vehicle dealers located within North Carolina, and which represents the collective interests of its members, shall have standing to file a petition before the Commissioner or a cause of action in any court of competent jurisdiction for itself, or on behalf of any or all of its members, seeking declaratory and injunctive relief. Prior to bringing an action, the association and captive finance source shall initiate mediation as set forth in G.S. 20-301.1(b). An action brought pursuant to this subsection may seek a determination whether one or more captive finance sources doing business in this State have violated any of the provisions of this Article, or for the determination of any rights created or defined by this Article, so long as the association alleges an injury to the collective interest of its members cognizable under this section. A cognizable injury to the collective interest of the members of the association shall be deemed to occur if a captive finance source doing business in this State has engaged in any conduct or taken any action which actually harms or affects all of the franchised new motor vehicle dealers holding agreements with that captive finance source in this State. With respect to any administrative or civil action filed by an association pursuant to this subsection, the relief granted shall be limited to declaratory and injunctive relief and in no event shall the Commissioner or court enter an award of monetary damages. (2005-409, s. 3.)

§ 20-308.22. Applicability of this Article.

(a) Any captive finance source who engages directly or indirectly in purposeful contacts within this State in connection with the offering or advertising the availability of financing for the sale or lease of motor vehicles within this State, or who has business dealings within this State, shall be subject to the provisions of this Article and shall be subject to the jurisdiction of the courts of this State.

(b) The applicability of this Article shall not be affected by a choice of law clause in any agreement, waiver, novation, or any other written instrument.

(c) Any provision of any agreement, waiver, novation, or any other written instrument which is in violation of any section of this Article shall be deemed null and void and without force and effect to the extent it violates this section.

(d) It shall be unlawful for a captive finance source to use any subsidiary corporation, affiliated corporation, or any other controlled corporation, partnership, association, or person to accomplish what would otherwise be illegal conduct under this Article on the part of the captive finance source. (2005-409, s. 3.)

Article 13.

The Vehicle Financial Responsibility Act of 1957.

§ 20-309. Financial responsibility prerequisite to registration; must be maintained throughout registration period.

(a) No motor vehicle shall be registered in this State unless the owner at the time of registration provides proof of financial responsibility for the operation of such motor vehicle, as provided in this Article. The owner of each motor vehicle registered in this State shall maintain financial responsibility continuously throughout the period of registration.

(a1) An owner of a commercial motor vehicle, as defined in G.S. 20-4.01(3d), shall have financial responsibility for the operation of the motor vehicle in an amount equal to that required for for-hire carriers transporting nonhazardous property in interstate or foreign commerce in 49 C.F.R. § 387.9.

(b) Financial responsibility shall be a liability insurance policy or a financial security bond or a financial security deposit or by qualification as a self-insurer, as these terms are defined and described in Article 9A, Chapter 20 of the General Statutes of North Carolina, as amended.

(c) When it is certified that financial responsibility is a liability insurance policy, the Commissioner of Motor Vehicles may require that the owner produce records to prove the fact of such insurance, and failure to produce such records shall be prima facie evidence that no financial responsibility exists with regard to the vehicle concerned. It shall be the duty of insurance companies, upon request of the Division, to verify the accuracy of any owner's certification.

(d) When liability insurance with regard to any motor vehicle is terminated by cancellation or failure to renew, or the owner's financial responsibility for the operation of any motor vehicle is otherwise terminated, the owner shall forthwith surrender the registration certificate and plates of the vehicle to the Division of Motor Vehicles unless financial responsibility is maintained in some other manner in compliance with this Article.

(e) Repealed by Session Laws 2006-213, s. 5, effective July 1, 2008, and applicable to lapses occurring on or after that date.

(f) The Commissioner shall administer and enforce the provisions of this Article and may make rules and regulations necessary for its administration and shall provide for hearings upon request of persons aggrieved by orders or acts of the Commissioner under the provisions of this Article.

(g) Repealed by Session Laws 2007-484, s. 7(a), effective July 1, 2008, and applicable to lapses occurring on or after that date.

(h) Recodified as G.S. 20-311(g) by Session Laws 2007-484, s. 7(d), effective July 1, 2008, and applicable to lapses occurring on or after that date. (1957, c. 1393, s. 1; 1959, c. 1277, s. 1; 1963, c. 964, s. 1; 1965, c. 272; c. 1136, ss. 1, 2; 1967, c. 822, ss. 1, 2; c. 857, ss. 1, 2; 1971, c. 477, ss. 1, 2; c. 924; 1975, c. 302; c. 348, ss. 1-3; c. 716, s. 5; 1979, 2nd Sess., c. 1279, s. 1; 1981, c. 690, s. 25; 1983, c. 761, s. 146; 1983 (Reg. Sess., 1984), c. 1069, ss. 1, 2; 1985, c. 666, s. 84; 1991, c. 402, s. 1; 1999-330, s. 4; 1999-452, s. 20; 2000-140, s. 100(a); 2000-155, s. 20; 2005-276, s. 6.37(p); 2006-213, s. 5; 2006-264, s. 38; 2007-484, ss. 7(a), (d); 2009-550, s. 4.)

§ 20-309.1: Repealed by Session Laws 1993 (Reg. Sess., 1994), c. 761, s. 28.

§ 20-309.2. Insurer shall notify Division of actions on insurance policies.

(a) Notice Required. - An insurer shall notify the Division upon any of the following with regard to a motor vehicle liability policy:

(1) Issues a new or replacement policy.

(2) Terminates a policy, either by cancellation or failure to renew, unless the same insurer issues a replacement policy complying with this Article at the same time the insurer terminates the old policy and no lapse in coverage results.

(3) Reinstates a policy after the insurer has notified the Division of a cancellation or termination.

(b) Time Period. - An insurer shall notify the Division as required by subsection (a) of this section within 20 business days.

(c) Form of Notice. - Any insurer with twenty-five million dollars ($25,000,000) or more in annual vehicle insurance premium volume shall submit the notices required under this section by electronic means. All other insurers may submit the notices required under this section by either paper or electronic means.

(d) Trade Secret Protection. - The names of insureds and the beginning date and termination date of insurance coverage provided to the Division by an insurer under this section constitutes a designated trade secret under G.S. 132-1.2.

(e) Civil Penalty. - The Commissioner of Insurance may assess a civil penalty of two hundred dollars ($200.00) against an insurer that fails to notify the Division as required by this section. The Commissioner may waive the penalty if the insurer establishes good cause for the failure.

(f) Clear Proceeds of Penalties. - The clear proceeds of all civil penalties, civil forfeitures, and civil fines that are collected by the Department of Transportation pursuant to this section shall be remitted to the Civil Penalty and Forfeiture Fund in accordance with G.S. 115C-457.2. (2006-213, s. 1; 2007-484, s. 7(b).)

§ 20-310: Repealed by Session Laws 1993 (Reg. Sess., 1994), c. 761, s. 29.

§ 20-310.1. Repealed by Session Laws 1963, c. 964, s. 3.

§ 20-310.2: Repealed by Session Laws 1993 (Reg. Sess., 1994), c. 761, s. 31.

§ 20-311. Action by the Division when notified of a lapse in financial responsibility.

(a) Action. - When the Division receives evidence, by a notice of termination of a motor vehicle liability policy or otherwise, that the owner of a motor vehicle registered or required to be registered in this State does not have financial responsibility for the operation of the vehicle, the Division shall send the owner a letter. The letter shall notify the owner of the evidence and inform the owner that the owner shall respond to the letter within 10 days of the date on the letter and explain how the owner has met the duty to have continuous financial responsibility for the vehicle. Based on the owner's response, the Division shall take the appropriate action listed:

(1) Division correction. - If the owner responds within the required time and the response establishes that the owner has not had a lapse in financial responsibility, the Division shall correct its records.

(2) Penalty only. - If the owner responds within the required time and the response establishes all of the following, the Division shall assess the owner a penalty in the amount set in subsection (b) of this section:

a. The owner had a lapse in financial responsibility, but the owner now has financial responsibility.

b. The vehicle was not involved in an accident during the lapse in financial responsibility.

c. The owner did not operate the vehicle during the lapse with knowledge that the owner had no financial responsibility for the vehicle.

(3) Penalty and revocation. - If the owner responds within the required time and the response establishes any of the following, the Division shall assess the owner a penalty in the amount set in subsection (b) of this section and revoke the registration of the owner's vehicle for the period set in subsection (c) of this section:

a. The owner had a lapse in financial responsibility and still does not have financial responsibility.

b. The owner now has financial responsibility even though the owner had a lapse, but the vehicle was involved in an accident during the lapse, the owner operated the vehicle during the lapse with knowledge that the owner had no financial responsibility for the vehicle, or both.

(4) Revocation pending response. - If the owner does not respond within the required time, the Division shall revoke the registration of the owner's vehicle for the period set in subsection (c) of this section. When the owner responds, the Division shall take the appropriate action listed in subdivisions (1) through (3) of this subsection as if the response had been timely.

(b) Penalty Amount. - The following table determines the amount of a penalty payable under this section by an owner who has had a lapse in financial responsibility; the amount is based on the number of times the owner has been assessed a penalty under this section during the three-year period before the date the owner's current lapse began:

Number of Lapses in Previous Three Years	Penalty Amount
None	$50.00
One	$100.00
Two or More	$150.00

(c) Revocation Period. - The revocation period for a revocation based on a response that establishes that a vehicle owner does not have financial responsibility is indefinite and ends when the owner obtains financial responsibility or transfers the vehicle to an owner who has financial responsibility. The revocation period for a revocation based on a response that establishes the occurrence of an accident during a lapse in financial responsibility or the knowing operation of a vehicle without financial responsibility is 30 days. The revocation period for a revocation based on failure of a vehicle owner to respond is indefinite and ends when the owner responds.

(d) Revocation Notice. - When the Division revokes the registration of an owner's vehicle, it shall notify the owner of the revocation. The notice shall inform the owner of the following:

(1) That the owner shall return the vehicle's registration plate and registration card to the Division, if the owner has not done so already, and that failure to do so is a Class 2 misdemeanor under G.S. 20-45.

(2) That the vehicle's registration plate and registration card are subject to seizure by a law enforcement officer.

(3) That the registration of the vehicle cannot be renewed while the registration is revoked.

(4) That the owner shall pay any penalties assessed, a restoration fee, and the fee for a registration plate when the owner applies to the Division to register a vehicle whose registration was revoked.

(e) Registration After Revocation. - A vehicle whose registration has been revoked may not be registered during the revocation period in the name of the owner, a child of the owner, the owner's spouse, or a child of the owner's spouse. This restriction does not apply to a spouse who is living separate and apart from the owner. At the end of a revocation period, a vehicle owner who has financial responsibility may apply to register a vehicle whose registration was revoked. The owner shall pay any penalty assessed, a restoration fee of fifty dollars ($50.00), and the fee for a registration plate.

(f) Clear Proceeds of Penalties. - The clear proceeds of all civil penalties, civil forfeitures, and civil fines that are collected by the Department of Transportation pursuant to this section shall be remitted to the Civil Penalty and Forfeiture Fund in accordance with G.S. 115C-457.2.

(g) Notwithstanding the penalty and restoration fee provisions of this section, any monetary penalty or restoration fee shall be waived for any person who, at the time of notification of a lapse in coverage, was deployed as a member of the Armed Forces of the United States outside of the continental United States for a total of 45 or more days. In addition, no insurance points under the Safe Driver Incentive Plan shall be assessed for any violation for which a monetary penalty or restoration fee is waived pursuant to this subsection. Any person qualifying under this subsection shall:

(1) Have an affirmative defense to any criminal charge based upon the failure to return any registration card or registration plate to the Division;

(2) Upon reregistration, receive without cost from the Division all necessary registration cards or plates; and

(3) Upon notice of revocation, be permitted to transfer the vehicle's registration immediately to his or her spouse, child, or spouse's child, notwithstanding the provisions of subsection (e) of this section. (1957, c. 1393, s. 3; 1959, c. 1277, s. 2; 1963, c. 964, s. 4; 1965, c. 205; c. 1136, s. 3; 1967, c. 822, s. 3; c. 857, s. 4; 1971, c. 477, s. 3; 1975, c. 348, s. 4; c. 716, s. 5; 1979, 2nd Sess., c. 1279, s. 2; 1983, c. 761, s. 147; 1983 (Reg. Sess., 1984), c. 1069, s. 2; 2006-213, s. 2; 2006-264, s. 38; 2007-484, ss. 7(c), (d); 2011-183, s. 24.)

§ 20-313. Operation of motor vehicle without financial responsibility a misdemeanor.

(a) On or after July 1, 1963, any owner of a motor vehicle registered or required to be registered in this State who shall operate or permit such motor vehicle to be operated in this State without having in full force and effect the financial responsibility required by this Article shall be guilty of a Class 3 misdemeanor.

(b) Evidence that the owner of a motor vehicle registered or required to be registered in this State has operated or permitted such motor vehicle to be operated in this State, coupled with proof of records of the Division of Motor Vehicles indicating that the owner did not have financial responsibility applicable to the operation of the motor vehicle in the manner certified by him for purposes of G.S. 20-309, shall be prima facie evidence that such owner did at the time and place alleged operate or permit such motor vehicle to be operated without having in full force and effect the financial responsibility required by the provisions of this Article. (1957, c. 1393, s. 5; 1959, c. 1277, s. 3; 1963, c. 964, s. 5; 1975, c. 716, s. 5; 1993, c. 539, s. 388; 1994, Ex. Sess., c. 24, s. 14(c); 2013-360, s. 18B.14(l).)

§ 20-313.1. Making false certification or giving false information a misdemeanor.

(a) Any owner of a motor vehicle registered or required to be registered in this State who shall make a false certification concerning his financial responsibility for the operation of such motor vehicle shall be guilty of a Class 1 misdemeanor.

(b) Any person, firm, or corporation giving false information to the Division concerning another's financial responsibility for the operation of a motor vehicle registered or required to be registered in this State, knowing or having reason to believe that such information is false, shall be guilty of a Class 1 misdemeanor. (1963, c. 964, s. 6; 1975, c. 716, s. 5; 1993, c. 539, s. 389; 1994, Ex. Sess., c. 24, s. 14(c).)

§ 20-314. Applicability of Article 9A; its provisions continued.

The provisions of Article 9A, Chapter 20 of the General Statutes, as amended, which pertain to the method of giving and maintaining proof of financial responsibility and which govern and define "motor vehicle liability policy" and assigned risk plans shall apply to filing and maintaining proof of financial responsibility required by this Article. It is intended that the provisions of Article 9A, Chapter 20 of the General Statutes, as amended, relating to proof of financial responsibility required of each operator and each owner of a motor vehicle involved in an accident, and relating to nonpayment of a judgment as defined in G.S. 20-279.1, shall continue in full force and effect. (1957, c. 1393, s. 6; 1963, c. 964, s. 7.)

§ 20-315. Commissioner to administer Article; rules and regulations.

The Commissioner of Motor Vehicles shall administer and enforce the provisions of this Article relating to registration of motor vehicles and may make necessary rules and regulations for its administration. (1957, c. 1393, s. 7.)

§ 20-316. Divisional hearings upon lapse of liability insurance coverage.

Any person whose registration plate has been revoked under G.S. 20-311 may request a hearing. Upon receipt of such request, the Division shall, as early as practical, afford an opportunity for hearing. At the hearing the duly authorized agents of the Division may administer oaths and issue subpoenas for the attendance of witnesses and the production of relevant books and documents. If it appears that continuous financial responsibility existed for the vehicle involved, or if it appears the lapse of financial responsibility is not reasonably attributable to the neglect or fault of the person whose registration plate was revoked, the Division shall withdraw its order of revocation and such person may retain the registration plate. Otherwise, the order of revocation shall be affirmed and the registration plate surrendered. (1971, c. 1218, s. 1; 1973, c. 1144, ss. 1, 2; 1975, c. 716, s. 5; 2006-213, s. 3.)

§ 20-316.1: Repealed by Session Laws 2006-213, s. 5, effective July 1, 2008, and applicable to lapses occurring on or after that date.

§ 20-317. Insurance required by any other law; certain operators not affected.

This Article shall not be held to apply to or affect policies of automobile insurance against liability which may now or hereafter be required by any other law of this State, and such policies, if they contain an agreement or are endorsed to conform to the requirements of this Article, may be certified as proof of financial responsibility under this Article. This Article applies to vehicles of motor carriers required to register with the Division under G.S. 20-382 or G.S. 20-382.1 only to the extent that the amount of financial responsibility required by this Article exceeds the amount required by the United States Department of Transportation. (1957, c. 1393, s. 9; 1959, c. 1252, s. 1; 1975, c. 716, s. 5; 1995 (Reg. Sess., 1996), c. 756, s. 19.)

§ 20-318. Federal, State and political subdivision vehicles excepted.

This Article does not apply to any motor vehicle owned by the State of North Carolina or by a political subdivision of the State, nor to any motor vehicle owned by the federal government. (1957, c. 1393, s. 10.)

§ 20-319. Effective date.

This Article shall be effective from and after January 1, 1958. (1957, c. 1393, s. 12; 1961, c. 276.)

Article 13A.

Certification of Automobile Insurance Coverage by Insurance Companies.

§ 20-319.1. Company to forward certification within seven days after receipt of request.

Upon the receipt by an insurance company at its home office of a registered letter from an insured requesting that it certify to the North Carolina Division of Motor Vehicles whether or not a previously issued policy of automobile liability insurance was in full force and effect on a designated day, it shall be the duty of such insurance company to forward such certification within seven days. (1967, c. 908, s. 1; 1975, c. 716, s. 5.)

§ 20-319.2. Penalty for failure to forward certification.

If any insurance company shall without good cause fail to forward said certification within seven days after its receipt of such registered letter, the North Carolina Commissioner of Insurance shall be authorized in his discretion to impose a civil penalty upon said company in the amount of two hundred dollars ($200.00) for such violation. (1967, c. 908, s. 2.)

Article 14.

Driver Training School Licensing Law.

§ 20-320. Definitions.

As used in this Article:

(1)   "Commercial driver training school" or "school" means a business enterprise conducted by an individual, association, partnership or corporation which educates or trains persons to operate or drive motor vehicles or which furnishes educational materials to prepare an applicant for an examination given by the State for a driver's license or learner's permit, and charges a consideration or tuition for such service or materials.

(2)   "Commissioner" means the Commissioner of Motor Vehicles.

(3)   "Instructor" means any person who operates a commercial driver training school or who teaches, conducts classes, gives demonstrations, or supervises practical training of persons learning to operate or drive motor vehicles in connection with operation of a commercial driver training school. (1965, c. 873; 1979, c. 667, s. 39.)

§ 20-321. Enforcement of Article by Commissioner.

(a)   The Commissioner shall adopt and prescribe such regulations concerning the administration and enforcement of this Article as are necessary to protect the public. The Commissioner or his authorized representative shall have the duty of examining applicants for commercial driver training schools and instructor's licenses, licensing successful applicants, and inspecting school facilities, records, and equipment.

(b)   The Commissioner shall administer and enforce the provisions of this Article, and may call upon the State Superintendent of Public Instruction for assistance in developing and formulating appropriate regulations. (1965, c. 873; 1973, c. 1331, s. 3; 1987, c. 69, c. 827, s. 3.)

§ 20-322. Licenses for schools necessary; regulations as to requirements.

(a)   No commercial driver training school shall be established nor any such existing school be continued on or after July 1, 1965, unless such school applies for and obtains from the Commissioner a license in the manner and form prescribed by the Commissioner.

(b)	Regulations adopted by the Commissioner shall state the requirements for a school license, including requirements concerning location, equipment, courses of instruction, instructors, financial statements, schedule of fees and charges, character and reputation of the operators, insurance, bond or other security in such sum and with such provisions as the Commissioner deems necessary to protect adequately the interests of the public, and such other matters as the Commissioner may prescribe. A driver education course offered to prepare an individual for a limited learner's permit or another provisional license must meet the requirements set in G.S. 115C-215 for the program of driver education offered in the public schools. (1965, c. 873; 1997-16, s. 4; 1997-443, s. 32.20; 2011-145, s. 28.37(e).)

§ 20-323. Licenses for instructors necessary; regulations as to requirements.

(a)	No person shall act as an instructor on or after July 1, 1965, unless such person applies for and obtains from the Commissioner a license in the manner and form prescribed by the Commissioner.

(b)	Regulations adopted by the Commissioner shall state the requirements for an instructor's license, including requirements concerning moral character, physical condition, knowledge of the courses of instruction, knowledge of the motor vehicle laws and safety principles, previous personal and employment records, and such other matters as the Commissioner may prescribe, for the protection of the public. (1965, c. 873.)

§ 20-324. Expiration and renewal of licenses; fees.

(a)	Renewal. - A license issued under this Article expires two years after the date the license is issued. To renew a license, the license holder must file an application for renewal with the Division.

(b)	Fees. - An application for an initial license or the renewal of a license must be accompanied by the application fee for the license. The application fee for a school license is eighty dollars ($80.00). The application fee for an instructor license is sixteen dollars ($16.00). The application fee for a license is not refundable. Fees collected under this section must be credited to the

Highway Fund. (1965, c. 873; 1977, c. 802, s. 9; 1981, c. 690, s. 15; 1997-33, s. 1.)

§ 20-325. Cancellation, suspension, revocation, and refusal to issue or renew licenses.

The Commissioner may cancel, suspend, revoke, or refuse to issue or renew a school or instructor's license in any case where he finds the licensee or applicant has not complied with, or has violated any of the provisions of this Article or any regulation adopted by the Commissioner hereunder. A suspended or revoked license shall be returned to the Commissioner by the licensee, and its holder shall not be eligible to apply for a license under this Article until 12 months have elapsed since the date of such suspension or revocation. (1965, c. 873.)

§ 20-326. Exemptions from Article.

The provisions of this Article shall not apply to any person giving driver training lessons without charge, to employers maintaining driver training schools without charge for their employees only, or to schools or classes conducted by colleges, universities and high schools. (1965, c. 873.)

§ 20-327. Penalties for violating Article or regulations.

Violation of any provision of this Article or any regulation promulgated pursuant hereto, shall constitute a Class 3 misdemeanor. (1965, c. 873; 1993, c. 539, s. 390; 1994, Ex. Sess., c. 24, s. 14(c).)

§ 20-328. Administration of Article.

This Article shall be administered by the Division of Motor Vehicles with no additional appropriations. (1965, c. 873; 1973, c. 440; 1975, c. 716, s. 5.)

§§ 20-329 through 20-339. Reserved for future codification purposes.

Article 15.

Vehicle Mileage Act.

§ 20-340. Purpose.

This Article shall provide State remedies for persons injured by motor vehicle odometer alteration, and to provide purchasers of motor vehicles with information to assist them in determining the condition and value of such vehicles. Such remedies shall be in addition to remedies provided by the federal odometer law (Motor Vehicle Information and Cost Savings Act, Public Law 92-513, 86 Stat. 947, enacted October 20, 1972). (1973, c. 679, s. 1.)

§ 20-341. Definitions.

As used in this Article:

(1) The term "odometer" means an instrument for measuring and recording the actual distance a motor vehicle travels while in operation; but shall not include any auxiliary odometer designed to be reset by the operator of the motor vehicle for the purpose of recording mileage on trips.

(2) The term "repair and replacement" means to restore to a sound working condition by replacing the odometer or any part thereof or by correcting what is inoperative.

(3) The term "transfer" means to change ownership by purchase, gift, or any other means.

(4) The term "transferee" means any person to whom the ownership in a motor vehicle is transferred or any person who, as agent, accepts transfer of ownership in a motor vehicle for another by purchase, gift, or any means other than by creation of a security interest.

(5) The term "transferor" means any person who or any person who, as agent, transfers his ownership in a motor vehicle by sale, gift or any means other than by creation of a security interest.

(6) The term "lessee" means any person, or the agent for any person, to whom a motor vehicle has been leased for a term of at least four months.

(7) The term "lessor" means any person, or the agent for any person, who has leased five or more vehicles in the past 12 months.

(8) The term "mileage" means the actual distance that a vehicle has traveled. (1973, c. 679, s. 1; 1989, c. 482, s. 1.)

§ 20-342. Unlawful devices.

It is unlawful for any person knowingly to advertise for sale, to sell, to use, or to install or to have installed, any device which causes an odometer to register any mileage other than the true mileage driven. For the purposes of this section, the true mileage driven is that mileage driven by the vehicle as registered by the odometer within the manufacturer's designed tolerance. (1973, c. 679, s. 1.)

§ 20-343. Unlawful change of mileage.

It is unlawful for any person or his agent to disconnect, reset, or alter the odometer of any motor vehicle with the intent to change the number of miles indicated thereon. Whenever evidence shall be presented in any court of the fact that an odometer has been reset or altered to change the number of miles indicated thereon, it shall be prima facie evidence in any court in the State of North Carolina that the resetting or alteration was made by the person, firm or corporation who held title or by law was required to hold title to the vehicle in which the reset or altered odometer was installed at the time of such resetting or alteration or if such person has more than 20 employees and has specifically and in writing delegated responsibility for the motor vehicle to an agent, that the resetting or alteration was made by the agent. (1973, c. 679, s. 1; 1979, c. 696.)

§ 20-344. Operation of vehicle with intent to defraud.

It is unlawful for any person with the intent to defraud to operate a motor vehicle on any street or highway knowing that the odometer of such vehicle is disconnected or nonfunctional. (1973, c. 679, s. 1.)

§ 20-345. Conspiracy.

No person shall conspire with any other person to violate G.S. 20-342, 20-343, 20-344, 20-346, 20-347, or 20-347.1. (1973, c. 679, s. 1; 1989, c. 482, s. 7.)

§ 20-346. Lawful service, repair, or replacement of odometer.

Nothing in this Article shall prevent the service, repair, or replacement of an odometer, provided the mileage indicated thereon remains the same as before the service, repair, or replacement. Where the odometer is incapable of registering the same mileage as before such service, repair, or replacement, the odometer shall be adjusted to read zero and a notice in writing shall be attached to the left door frame of the vehicle by the owner or his agent specifying the mileage prior to repair or replacement of the odometer and the date on which it was repaired or replaced. Any removal or alteration of such notice so affixed shall be unlawful. (1973, c. 679, s. 1.)

§ 20-347. Disclosure requirements.

(a)   In connection with the transfer of a motor vehicle, the transferor shall disclose the mileage to the transferee in writing on the title or on the document used to reassign the title. This written disclosure must be signed by the transferor, including the printed name, and shall contain the following information:

(1)   The odometer reading at the time of the transfer (not to include tenths of miles);

(2) The date of the transfer;

(3) The transferor's name and current address;

(3a) The transferee's printed name, signature and current address;

(4) The identity of the vehicle, including its make, model, body type, and vehicle identification number, and the license plate number most recently used on the vehicle; and

(5) Certification by the transferor that to the best of his knowledge the odometer reading

a. Reflects the actual mileage; or

b. Reflects the amount of mileage in excess of the designed mechanical odometer limit; or

c. Does not reflect the actual mileage and should not be relied on.

(6), (7) Repealed by Session Laws 1989, c. 482, s. 2.

(a1) Before executing any transfer of ownership document, each lessor of a leased motor vehicle shall notify the lessee in writing that the lessee is required to provide written disclosure to the lessor regarding mileage. In connection with the transfer of ownership of the leased motor vehicle, the lessee shall furnish to the lessor a written statement signed by the lessee containing the following information:

(1) The printed name of the person making the disclosure;

(2) The current odometer reading (not to include tenths of miles);

(3) The date of the statement;

(4) The lessee's printed name and current address;

(5) The lessor's printed name, signature, and current address;

(6) The identity of the vehicle, including its make, model, year, body type, and vehicle identification number;

(7) The date that the lessor notified the lessee of the disclosure requirements and the date the lessor received the completed disclosure statement; and

(8) Certification by the lessee that to the best of his knowledge the odometer reading:

a. Reflects the actual mileage;

b. Reflects the amount of mileage in excess of the designed mechanical odometer limit; or

c. Does not reflect the actual mileage and should not be relied on.

If the lessor transfers the leased vehicle without obtaining possession of it, the lessor may indicate on the title the mileage disclosed by the lessee under this subsection, unless the lessor has reason to believe that the disclosure by the lessee does not reflect the actual mileage of the vehicle.

(b) Repealed by Session Laws 1973, c. 1088.

(c) It shall be unlawful for any transferor to violate any rules under this section or to knowingly give a false statement to a transferee in making any disclosure required by such rules.

(d) The provisions of this disclosure statement section shall not apply to the following transfers:

(1) A vehicle having a gross vehicle weight rating of more than 16,000 pounds.

(2) A vehicle that is not self-propelled.

(2a) A vehicle sold directly by the manufacturer to any agency of the United States in conformity with contractual specifications.

(3) A vehicle that is 10 years old or older.

(4) A new vehicle prior to its first transfer for purposes other than resale.

(5) A vehicle that is transferred by a State agency that assists the United States Department of Defense with purchasing, transferring, or titling a vehicle to another State agency, a unit of local government, a volunteer fire department, or a volunteer rescue squad. (1973, c. 679, s. 1; c. 1088; 1983, c. 387; 1989, c. 482, ss. 2-5; 1993, c. 553, s. 11; 2009-550, s. 2(d).)

§ 20-347.1. Odometer disclosure record retention.

(a) Dealers and distributors of motor vehicles who are required by this Part to execute an odometer disclosure statement shall retain, for five years, a photostat, carbon, or other facsimile copy of each odometer mileage statement which they issue or receive. They shall retain all odometer disclosure statements at their primary place of business in an order that is appropriate to business requirements and that permits systematic retrieval.

(b) Lessors shall retain, for five years following the date they transfer ownership of the leased vehicle, each odometer disclosure statement which they receive from a lessee. They shall retain all odometer disclosure statements at their primary place of business in an order that is appropriate to business requirements and that permits systematic retrieval.

(c) Each auction company shall establish and retain at its primary place of business in an order that is appropriate to business requirements and that permits systematic retrieval, for five years following the date of sale of each motor vehicle, the following records:

(1) The name of the most recent owner (other than the auction company);

(2) The name of the buyer;

(3) The vehicle identification number; and

(4) The odometer reading on the date which the auction company took possession of the motor vehicle.

(d) Records required to be kept under this section shall be open to inspection and copying by law enforcement officers of the Division in order to determine compliance with this Article. (1989, c. 482, s. 6.)

§ 20-348. Private civil action.

(a) Any person who, with intent to defraud, violates any requirement imposed under this Article shall be liable in an amount equal to the sum of:

(1) Three times the amount of actual damages sustained or one thousand five hundred dollars ($1,500), whichever is the greater; and

(2) In the case of any successful action to enforce the foregoing liability, the costs of the action together with reasonable attorney fees as determined by the court.

(b) An action to enforce any liability created under subsection (a) of this section may be brought in any court of the trial division of the General Court of Justice of the State of North Carolina within four years from the date on which the liability arises. (1973, c. 679, s. 1; 1981 (Reg. Sess., 1982), c. 1280, s. 1.)

§ 20-349. Injunctive enforcement.

Upon petition by the Attorney General of North Carolina, a violation of this Article may be enjoined as an unfair and deceptive trade practice, as prohibited by G.S. 75-1.1. (1973, c. 679, s. 1.)

§ 20-350. Criminal offense.

Any person, firm or corporation violating G.S. 20-343 shall be guilty of a Class I felony. A violation of any remaining provision of this Article shall be a Class 1 misdemeanor. (1973, c. 679, s. 1; 1989, c. 482, s. 7.1; 1993, c. 539, ss. 391, 1262; 1994, Ex. Sess., c. 24, s. 14(c).)

Article 15A.

New Motor Vehicles Warranties Act.

§ 20-351. Purpose.

This Article shall provide State and private remedies against motor vehicle manufacturers for persons injured by new motor vehicles failing to conform to express warranties. (1987, c. 385, s. 1.)

§ 20-351.1. Definitions.

As used in this Article:

(1) "Consumer" means the purchaser, other than for purposes of resale, or lessee from a commercial lender, lessor, or from a manufacturer or dealer, of a motor vehicle, and any other person entitled by the terms of an express warranty to enforce the obligations of that warranty.

(2) "Manufacturer" means any person or corporation, resident or nonresident, who manufactures or assembles or imports or distributes new motor vehicles which are sold in the State of North Carolina.

(3) "Motor vehicle" includes a motor vehicle as defined in G.S. 20-4.01 that is sold or leased in this State, but does not include "house trailer" as defined in G.S. 20-4.01 or any motor vehicle that weighs more than 10,000 pounds.

(4) "New motor vehicle" means a motor vehicle for which a certificate of origin, as required by G.S. 20-52.1 or a similar requirement in another state, has never been supplied to a consumer, or which a manufacturer, its agent, or its authorized dealer states in writing is being sold as a new motor vehicle. (1987, c. 385, s. 1; 1989, c. 43, s. 2; c. 519, s. 2; 2005-436, s. 1.)

§ 20-351.2. Require repairs; when mileage warranty begins to accrue.

(a) Express warranties for a new motor vehicle shall remain in effect at least one year or 12,000 miles. If a new motor vehicle does not conform to all applicable express warranties for a period of one year, or the term of the express warranties, whichever is greater, following the date of original delivery of the motor vehicle to the consumer, and the consumer reports the nonconformity to the manufacturer, its agent, or its authorized dealer during such period, the manufacturer shall make, or arrange to have made, repairs necessary to conform the vehicle to the express warranties, whether or not these repairs are made after the expiration of the applicable warranty period.

(b) Any express warranty for a new motor vehicle expressed in terms of a certain number of miles shall begin to accrue from the mileage on the odometer at the date of original delivery to the consumer. (1987, c. 385; 1989, c. 14.)

§ 20-351.3. Replacement or refund; disclosure requirement.

(a) When the consumer is the purchaser or a person entitled by the terms of the express warranty to enforce the obligations of the warranty, if the manufacturer is unable, after a reasonable number of attempts, to conform the motor vehicle to any express warranty by repairing or correcting, or arranging for the repair or correction of, any defect or condition or series of defects or conditions which substantially impair the value of the motor vehicle to the consumer, and which occurred no later than 24 months or 24,000 miles following original delivery of the vehicle, the manufacturer shall, at the option of the consumer, replace the vehicle with a comparable new motor vehicle or accept return of the vehicle from the consumer and refund to the consumer the following:

(1) The full contract price including, but not limited to, charges for undercoating, dealer preparation and transportation, and installed options, plus the non-refundable portions of extended warranties and service contracts;

(2) All collateral charges, including but not limited to, sales tax, license and registration fees, and similar government charges;

(3) All finance charges incurred by the consumer after he first reports the nonconformity to the manufacturer, its agent, or its authorized dealer; and

(4) Any incidental damages and monetary consequential damages.

(b) When consumer is a lessee, if the manufacturer is unable, after a reasonable number of attempts, to conform the motor vehicle to any express warranty by repairing or correcting, or arranging for the repair or correction of, any defect or condition or series of defects or conditions which substantially impair the value of the motor vehicle to the consumer, and which occurred no later than 24 months or 24,000 miles following original delivery of the vehicle, the manufacturer shall, at the option of the consumer, replace the vehicle with a comparable new motor vehicle or accept return of the vehicle from the consumer and refund the following:

(1) To the consumer:

a. All sums previously paid by the consumer under the terms of the lease;

b. All sums previously paid by the consumer in connection with entering into the lease agreement, including, but not limited to, any capitalized cost reduction, sales tax, license and registration fees, and similar government charges; and

c. Any incidental and monetary consequential damages.

(2) To the lessor, a full refund of the lease price, plus an additional amount equal to five percent (5%) of the lease price, less eighty-five percent (85%) of the amount actually paid by the consumer to the lessor pursuant to the lease. The lease price means the actual purchase cost of the vehicle to the lessor.

In the case of a refund, the leased vehicle shall be returned to the manufacturer and the consumer's written lease shall be terminated by the lessor without any penalty to the consumer. The lessor shall transfer title of the motor vehicle to the manufacturer as necessary to effectuate the consumer's rights pursuant to this Article, whether the consumer chooses vehicle replacement or refund.

(c) Refunds shall be made to the consumer, lessor, and any lienholders as their interests may appear. The refund to the consumer shall be reduced by a reasonable allowance for the consumer's use of the vehicle. A reasonable allowance for use is calculated from the number of miles used by the consumer up to the date of the third attempt to repair the same nonconformity which is the subject of the claim, or the twentieth cumulative business day when the vehicle is out of service by reason of repair of one or more nonconformities, whichever occurs first. The number of miles used by the consumer is multiplied by the purchase price of the vehicle or the lessor's actual lease price, and divided by 120,000.

(d) If a manufacturer, its agent, or its authorized dealer resells a motor vehicle that was returned pursuant to this Article or any other State's applicable law, regardless of whether there was any judicial determination that the motor vehicle had any defect or that it failed to conform to all express warranties, the manufacturer, its agent, or its authorized dealer shall disclose to the subsequent purchaser prior to the sale:

(1)   That the motor vehicle was returned pursuant to this Article or pursuant to the applicable law of any other State; and

(2)   The defect or condition or series of defects or conditions which substantially impaired the value of the motor vehicle to the consumer.

Any subsequent purchaser who purchases the motor vehicle for resale with notice of the return, shall make the required disclosures to any person to whom he resells the motor vehicle. (1987, c. 385, s. 1; 1989, c. 43, s. 1; c. 519, s. 1; 2005-436, s. 2.)

§ 20-351.4. Affirmative defenses.

It is an affirmative defense to any claim under this Article that an alleged nonconformity or series of nonconformities are the result of abuse, neglect, odometer tampering by the consumer or unauthorized modifications or alterations of a motor vehicle. (1987, c. 385.)

§ 20-351.5. Presumption.

(a)   It is presumed that a reasonable number of attempts have been undertaken to conform a motor vehicle to the applicable express warranties if:

(1)   The same nonconformity has been presented for repair to the manufacturer, its agent, or its authorized dealer four or more times but the same nonconformity continues to exist; or

(2)   The vehicle was out of service to the consumer during or while awaiting repair of the nonconformity or a series of nonconformities for a cumulative total of 20 or more business days during any 12-month period of the warranty,

provided that the consumer has notified the manufacturer directly in writing of the existence of the nonconformity or series of nonconformities and allowed the manufacturer a reasonable period, not to exceed 15 calendar days, in which to correct the nonconformity or series of nonconformities. The manufacturer must clearly and conspicuously disclose to the consumer in the warranty or owners manual that written notification of a nonconformity is required before a consumer may be eligible for a refund or replacement of the vehicle and the manufacturer shall include in the warranty or owners manual the name and address where the written notification may be sent. Provided, further, that notice to the manufacturer shall not be required if the manufacturer fails to make the disclosures provided herein.

(b) The consumer may prove that a defect or condition substantially impairs the value of the motor vehicle to the consumer in a manner other than that set forth in subsection (a) of this section.

(c) The term of an express warranty, the one-year period, and the 20-day period shall be extended by any period of time during which repair services are not available to the consumer because of war, strike, or natural disaster. (1987, c. 385.)

§ 20-351.6. Civil action by the Attorney General.

Whenever, in his opinion, the interests of the public require it, it shall be the duty of the Attorney General upon his ascertaining that any of the provisions of this Article have been violated by the manufacturer to bring a civil action in the name of the State, or any officer or department thereof as provided by law, or in the name of the State on relation of the Attorney General. (1987, c. 385, s. 1.)

§ 20-351.7. Civil action by the consumer.

A consumer injured by reason of any violation of the provisions of this Article may bring a civil action against the manufacturer; provided, however, the consumer has given the manufacturer written notice of his intent to bring an action against the manufacturer at least 10 days prior to filing such suit. Nothing in this section shall prevent a manufacturer from requiring a consumer to utilize an informal settlement procedure prior to litigation if that procedure substantially complies in design and operation with the Magnuson-Moss Warranty Act, 15 USC § 2301 et seq., and regulations promulgated thereunder, and that requirement is written clearly and conspicuously, in the written warranty and any warranty instructions provided to the consumer. (1987, c. 385, s. 1.)

§ 20-351.8. Remedies.

In any action brought under this Article, the court may grant as relief:

(1) A permanent or temporary injunction or other equitable relief as the court deems just;

(2) Monetary damages to the injured consumer in the amount fixed by the verdict. Such damages shall be trebled upon a finding that the manufacturer unreasonably refused to comply with G.S. 20-351.2 or G.S. 20-351.3. The jury may consider as damages all items listed for refund under G.S. 20-351.3;

(3) A reasonable attorney's fee for the attorney of the prevailing party, payable by the losing party, upon a finding by the court that:

a. The manufacturer unreasonably failed or refused to fully resolve the matter which constitutes the basis of such action; or

b. The party instituting the action knew, or should have known, the action was frivolous and malicious. (1987, c. 385.)

§ 20-351.9. Dealership liability.

No authorized dealer shall be held liable by the manufacturer for any refunds or vehicle replacements in the absence of evidence indicating that dealership repairs have been carried out in a manner substantially inconsistent with the manufacturers' instructions. This Article does not create any cause of action by a consumer against an authorized dealer. (1987, c. 385.)

§ 20-351.10. Preservation of other remedies.

This Article does not limit the rights or remedies which are otherwise available to a consumer under any other law. (1987, c. 385.)

§ 20-351.11. Manufacturer's warranty for State motor vehicles that operate on diesel fuel.

Every new motor vehicle purchased by the State that is designed to operate on diesel fuel shall be covered by an express manufacturer's warranty that allows the use of B-20 fuel, as defined in G.S. 143-58.4. This section does not apply if the intended use, as determined by the agency, of the new motor vehicle requires a type of vehicle for which an express manufacturer's warranty allows the use of B-20 fuel is not available. (2007-420, s. 1.)

§ 20-352. Reserved for future codification purposes.

§ 20-353. Reserved for future codification purposes.

Article 15B.

North Carolina Motor Vehicle Repair Act.

§ 20-354. Short title.

This act shall be known and may be cited as the "North Carolina Motor Vehicle Repair Act." (1999-437, s. 1.)

§ 20-354.1. Scope and application.

This act shall apply to all motor vehicle repair shops in North Carolina, except:

(1) Any motor vehicle repair shop of a municipal, county, State, or federal government when carrying out the functions of the government.

(2) Any person who engages solely in the repair of any of the following:

a. Motor vehicles that are owned, maintained, and operated exclusively by that person for that person's own use.

b. For-hire vehicles which are rented for periods of 30 days or less.

(3) Any person who repairs only motor vehicles which are operated principally for agricultural or horticultural pursuits on farms, groves, or orchards and which are operated on the highways of this State only incidentally en route to or from the farms, groves, or orchards.

(4) Motor vehicle auctions or persons in the performance of motor vehicle repairs solely for motor vehicle auctions.

(5) Any motor vehicle repair shop in the performance of a motor vehicle repair if the cost of the repair does not exceed three hundred fifty dollars ($350.00).

(6) Any person or motor vehicle repair shop in the performance of repairs on commercial construction equipment or motor vehicles that have a GVWR of at least 26,001 pounds.

(7) When a third party has waived in writing the right to receive written estimates from the motor vehicle repair shop; the third party indicates to the motor vehicle repair shop that the repairs will be paid for by the third party under an insurance policy, service contract, mechanical breakdown contract, or manufacturer's warranty; and the third party further indicates that the customer's share of the cost of repairs, if any, will not exceed three hundred fifty dollars ($350.00). (1999-437, s. 1; 2001-298, s. 1.)

§ 20-354.2. Definitions.

As used in this act:

(1) "Customer" means the person who signs the written repair estimate or any other person whom that person designates as a person who may authorize repair work.

(2) "Employee" means an individual who is employed full time or part time by a motor vehicle repair shop and performs motor vehicle repairs.

(3) "Motor vehicle" means any automobile, truck, bus, recreational vehicle, motorcycle, motor scooter, or other motor-powered vehicle, but does not include trailers, mobile homes, travel trailers, or trailer coaches without independent motive power, or watercraft or aircraft.

(4) "Motor vehicle repair" means all maintenance of and modification and repairs to motor vehicles and the diagnostic work incident to those repairs, including, but not limited to, the rebuilding or restoring of rebuilt vehicles, body work, painting, warranty work, shop supply fees, hazardous material disposal fees incident to a repair, and other work customarily undertaken by motor vehicle repair shops. Motor vehicle repair does not include the sale or installation of tires when authorized by the customer.

(5) "Motor vehicle repair shop" means any person who, for compensation, engages or attempts to engage in the repair of motor vehicles owned by other persons and includes, but is not limited to:

a. Mobile motor vehicle repair shops.

b. Motor vehicle and recreational vehicle dealers.

c. Garages.

d. Service stations.

e. Self-employed individuals.

f. Truck stops.

g. Paint and body shops.

h. Brake, muffler, or transmission shops.

i. Shops doing glasswork.

Any person who engages solely in the maintenance or repair of the coach portion of a recreational vehicle is not a motor vehicle repair shop. (1999-437, s. 1; 2005-463, s. 1.)

§ 20-354.3. Written motor vehicle repair estimate and disclosure statement required.

(a) When any customer requests a motor vehicle repair shop to perform repair work on a motor vehicle, the cost of which repair work will exceed three hundred fifty dollars ($350.00) to the customer, the shop shall prepare a written repair estimate, which is a form setting forth the estimated cost of repair work, including diagnostic work, before effecting any diagnostic work or repair. In determining under this section whether the cost of the repair work exceeds three hundred fifty dollars ($350.00), the cost of the repair work shall consist of the cost of parts and labor necessary for the repair work and any charges for necessary diagnostic work and teardown, if any, and shall include any taxes, any other repair shop supplies or overhead, and any other extra services that are incidental to the repair work. The written repair estimate shall also include a statement allowing the customer to indicate whether replaced parts should be saved for inspection or return and a statement indicating the daily charge for storing the customer's motor vehicle after the customer has been notified that the repair work has been completed.

(b) The information required by subsection (a) of this section need not be provided if the customer waives in writing his or her right to receive a written estimate. A customer may waive his or her right to receive any written estimates from a motor vehicle repair shop for a period of time specified by the customer in the waiver.

(c) Except as provided in subsection (e) of this section, a copy of the written repair estimate required by subsection (a) of this section shall be given to the customer before repair work is begun.

(d) If the customer leaves his or her motor vehicle at a motor vehicle repair shop during hours when the shop is not open, or if the motor vehicle repair shop reasonably believes that an accurate estimate of the cost of repairs cannot be made until after the diagnostic work has been completed, or if the customer permits the shop or another person to deliver the motor vehicle to the shop, there shall be an implied partial waiver of the written estimate; however, upon completion of the diagnostic work necessary to estimate the cost of repair, the shop shall notify the customer as required by G.S. 20-354.5(a).

(e) Nothing in this section shall be construed to require a motor vehicle repair shop to give a written estimate price if the motor vehicle repair shop does not agree to perform the requested repair. (1999-437, s. 1; 2001-298, s. 2; 2005-304, s. 1.)

§ 20-354.4. Charges for motor vehicle repair estimate; requirement of waiver of rights prohibited.

(a) Before proceeding with preparing an estimate, the shop shall do both of the following:

(1) Disclose to the customer the amount, if any, of the charge for preparing the estimate.

(2) Obtain a written authorization to prepare an estimate if there is a charge for that estimate.

(b) It is a violation of this Article for any motor vehicle repair shop to require that any person waive his or her rights provided in this Article as a precondition to the repair of his or her vehicle by the shop or to impose or threaten to impose any charge which is clearly excessive in relation to the work involved in making the price estimate for the purpose of inducing the customer to waive his or her rights provided in this Article. (1999-437, s. 1.)

§ 20-354.5. Notification of charges in excess of repair estimate; prohibited charges; refusal to return vehicle prohibited; inspection of parts.

(a) In the event that any of the following applies, the customer shall be promptly notified by telephone, telegraph, mail, or other means of the additional repair work and estimated cost of the additional repair work:

(1) The written repair estimate contains only an estimate for diagnostic work necessary to estimate the cost of repair and such diagnostic work has been completed.

(2) A determination is made by a motor vehicle repair shop that the actual charges for the repair work will exceed the written estimate by more than ten percent (10%).

(3) An implied partial waiver exists for diagnostic work, and the diagnostic work has been completed.

When a customer is notified, he or she shall, orally or in writing, authorize, modify, or cancel the order for repair.

(b) If a customer cancels the order for repair or, after diagnostic work is performed, decides not to have the repairs performed, and if the customer authorizes the motor vehicle repair shop to reassemble the motor vehicle, the shop shall expeditiously reassemble the motor vehicle in a condition reasonably similar to the condition in which it was received.

After cancellation of the repair order or a decision by the customer not to have repairs made after diagnostic work has been performed, the shop may charge for and the customer is obligated to pay the cost of repairs actually completed that were authorized by the written repair estimate as well as the cost of diagnostic work and teardown, the cost of parts and labor to replace items that were destroyed by teardown, and the cost to reassemble the component or the vehicle, provided the customer was notified of these possible costs in the written repair estimate or at the time the customer authorized the motor vehicle repair shop to reassemble the motor vehicle.

(c) It is a violation of this Article for a motor vehicle repair shop to charge more than the written estimate and the amount by which the motor vehicle repair shop has obtained authorization to exceed the written estimate in accordance with subsections (a) or (b) of this section, plus ten percent (10%).

(d) It is a violation of this Article for any motor vehicle repair shop to refuse to return any customer's motor vehicle because the customer refused to pay for repair charges that exceed a written estimate and any amounts authorized by the customer in accordance with subsection (a) or (b) of this section by more than ten percent (10%), provided that the customer has paid the motor vehicle repair shop the amount of the estimate and the amounts authorized by the customer in accordance with subsections (a) and (b) of this section, plus ten percent (10%).

(e) Upon request made at the time the repair work is authorized by the customer, the customer is entitled to inspect parts removed from his or her vehicle or, if the shop has no warranty arrangement or exchange parts program with a manufacturer, supplier, or distributor, have them returned to him or her. A motor vehicle repair shop may discard parts removed from a customer's vehicle or sell them and retain the proceeds for the shop's own account if the customer fails to take possession of the parts at the shop within two business days after taking delivery of the repaired vehicle. (1999-437, s. 1; 2001-298, ss. 3, 4.)

§ 20-354.6. Invoice required of motor vehicle repair shop.

The motor vehicle repair shop shall provide each customer, upon completion of any repair, with a legible copy of an invoice for such repair. The invoice shall include the following information:

(1) A statement indicating what was done to correct the problem or a description of the service provided.

(2) An itemized description of all labor, parts, and merchandise supplied and the costs of all labor, parts, and merchandise supplied. No itemized description is required to be provided to the customer for labor, parts, and merchandise supplied when a third party has indicated to the motor vehicle repair shop that the repairs will be paid for under a service contract, under a mechanical breakdown contract, or under a manufacturer's warranty, without charge to the customer.

(3) A statement identifying any replacement part as being used, rebuilt, or reconditioned, as the case may be. (1999-437, s. 1; 2001-298, s. 5; 2002-159, s. 32.)

§ 20-354.7. Required disclosure; signs; notice to customers.

A sign, at least 24 inches on each side, shall be posted in a manner conspicuous to the public. The sign shall contain:

(1) That the consumer has a right to receive a written estimate or to waive receipt of that estimate if the cost of repairs will exceed three hundred fifty dollars ($350.00).

(2) That the consumer may request, at the time the work order is taken, the return or inspection of all parts that have been replaced during the motor vehicle repair. (1999-437, s. 1.)

§ 20-354.8. Prohibited acts and practices.

It shall be a violation of this Article for any motor vehicle repair shop or employee of a motor vehicle repair shop to do any of the following:

(1) Charge for repairs which have not been expressly or impliedly authorized by the customer.

(2) Misrepresent that repairs have been made to a motor vehicle.

(3) Misrepresent that certain parts and repairs are necessary to repair a vehicle.

(4) Misrepresent that the vehicle being inspected or diagnosed is in a dangerous condition or that the customer's continued use of the vehicle may be harmful or cause great damage to the vehicle.

(5) Fraudulently alter any customer contract, estimate, invoice, or other document.

(6) Fraudulently misuse any customer's credit card.

(7) Make or authorize in any manner or by any means whatever any written or oral statement which is untrue, deceptive, or misleading, and which is known, or which by the exercise of reasonable care should be known, to be untrue, deceptive, or misleading, related to this Article.

(8) Make fraudulent promises of a character likely to influence, persuade, or induce a customer to authorize the repair, service, or maintenance of a motor vehicle.

(9) Substitute used, rebuilt, salvaged, or straightened parts for new replacement parts without notice to the motor vehicle owner and to his or her insurer if the cost of repair is to be paid pursuant to an insurance policy and the identity of the insurer or its claims adjuster is disclosed to the motor vehicle repair shop.

(10) Cause or allow a customer to sign any work order that does not state the repairs requested by the customer.

(11) Refuse to give to a customer a copy of any document requiring the customer's signature upon completion or cancellation of the repair work.

(12) Rebuild or restore a rebuilt vehicle without the knowledge of the owner in a manner that does not conform to the original vehicle manufacturer's established repair procedures or specifications and allowable tolerances for the particular model and year.

(13) Perform any other act that is a violation of this Article or that constitutes fraud or misrepresentation under this Article. (1999-437, s. 1.)

§ 20-354.9. Remedies.

Any customer injured by a violation of this Article may bring an action in the appropriate court for relief. The prevailing party in that action may be entitled to damages plus court costs and reasonable attorneys' fees. The customer may also bring an action for injunctive relief in the appropriate court. A violation of this Article is not punishable as a crime; however, this Article does not limit the rights or remedies which are otherwise available to a consumer under any other law. (1999-437, s. 1.)

§§ 20-354.10 through 20-355. Reserved for future codification purposes.

Article 16.

Professional Housemoving.

§ 20-356. Definitions.

As used in this Article, the following terms mean:

(1) Department. - The Department of Transportation.

(2) House. - A dwelling, building, or other structure in excess of 15 feet in width. Mobile homes, manufactured homes, or modular homes, or portions thereof, are not within this definition when being transported from the manufacturer or from a licensed retail dealer location to the first set-up site.

(3) Housemover. - A person licensed under this Article.

(4) Person. - An individual, corporation, partnership, association, or any other business entity.

(5) Secretary. - The Secretary of the Department of Transportation.

(6) Unsafe practices. - Any act that is determined by a final agency decision of an enforcing agency or by a court of competent jurisdiction to create a hazard to the motoring public, or any citations under the Occupational Safety and Health Act that have become a final order within the last three years for willful serious violations or for failing to abate serious violations, as defined in G.S. 95-127. (1977, c. 720, s. 1; 1979, c. 475, s. 2; 2001-424, s. 27.17(a); 2005-354, s. 1; 2008-89, s. 1.)

§ 20-357. Housemovers to be licensed.

All persons who engage in the profession of housemoving on roads and highways on the State Highway System shall be licensed by the Department. (1977, c. 720, s. 2.)

§ 20-358. Qualifications to become licensed.

The Department shall issue annual printed licenses to applicants meeting the following conditions:

(1) The applicant must be at least 21 years of age; present acceptable evidence of good character and show sufficient housemoving experience on the application form furnished by the Department. Proof of creditable housemoving experience must be furnished at the time of application for those applicants not previously licensed by the Department. Creditable housemoving experience means extensive and responsible training gained by the applicant while engaged actively and directly on a full-time basis in the moving of houses and structures on public roads and highways with at least five years of experience. Examples of the capacity in which a person may work in gaining experience include the following in building moving operations:

a. Moving superintendent,

b. Moving foreman, and

c. General mechanic and helper in the housemoving profession or trade.

To comply with the requirement of proof of creditable housemoving experience, each applicant not previously licensed under this Article shall submit to the Department an affidavit from a certified public accountant that the applicant has documented employment records for a period of five continuous years from a person or persons licensed by this State or another state for housemoving. Each applicant not previously licensed under this Article shall also submit to the Department affidavits from a person or persons licensed in this State or another state in housemoving, who have employed the applicant in housemoving, providing in detail the applicant's full-time experience, including any supervisory duties and experience, in housemoving.

(2) Repealed by Session Laws 1981, c. 818, s. 3.

(3) The applicant must furnish proof that all of the vehicles, excluding "beams and dollies" and "hauling units," to be used in the movement of buildings, structures, or other extraordinary objects wider than 15 feet have met the requirements of G.S. 20-183.2 pertaining to the equipment inspection of motor vehicles; provided that the "beams and dollies" and "hauling units" are excluded from inspection under G.S. 20-183.2 and, further, are not required to be equipped with brakes.

(4) The applicant must exhibit his federal employer's identification number.

(5) The applicant must pay an annual license fee of one hundred dollars ($100.00). (1977, c. 720, s. 3; 1981, c. 818, s. 3; 1991 (Reg. Sess., 1992), c. 813, s. 2; 2005-354, s. 2; 2008-89, s. 2.)

§ 20-359. Effective period of license.

A license issued hereunder shall be effective from date of issuance and expire on July 31 of each year and shall be renewable on an annual basis. (1977, c. 720, s. 4; 2005-354, s. 3.)

§ 20-359.1. Insurance requirements.

(a) No license shall be issued or renewed pursuant to this Article unless the applicant files with the Department a certificate or certificates of insurance, from an insurance company or companies authorized to do business in this State, providing:

(1) Motor vehicle insurance for bodily injury to or death of one or more persons in any one accident and for injury to or destruction of property of others in any one accident with minimum coverage of three hundred fifty thousand dollars ($350,000) combined single limit of liability;

(2) Comprehensive general liability insurance with a minimum coverage of three hundred fifty thousand dollars ($350,000) combined single limit of liability, including coverage of operations on North Carolina streets and highways that are not covered by motor vehicle insurance; and

(3) Workers' compensation insurance that complies with Chapter 97 for all employees if the person is licensed as a professional housemover. The exemptions in G.S. 97-13 from the provisions of Chapter 97 shall not apply to licensed professional housemovers.

(b) The certificate or certificates shall provide for continuous coverage during the effective period of the license issued pursuant to this Article. At the time the certificate is filed, the applicant shall also file with the Department a current list of all motor vehicles covered by the certificate. The applicant shall file amendments to the list within 15 days of any changes.

(c)   An insurance company issuing any insurance policy required by subsection (a) of this section shall notify the Department of any of the following events at least 30 days before its occurrence: (i) cancellation of the policy, (ii) nonrenewal of the policy, or (iii) any change in the policy.

(d)   In addition to all coverages required by this section, the applicant shall file with the Department a copy of either: (i) a bond or other acceptable surety providing coverage in the amount of twenty-five thousand dollars ($25,000) for the benefit of a person contracting with the housemover to move that person's structure for all claims for property damage arising from the movement of a structure pursuant to this Article, or (ii) a policy of cargo insurance in the amount of fifty thousand dollars ($50,000). (1981, c. 818, s. 1; 1991 (Reg. Sess., 1992), c. 813, s. 1.)

§ 20-360. Requirements for permit.

(a)   Persons licensed as professional housemovers shall also be required to secure a permit from the Department for every move undertaken on the State Highway System of roads; that permit shall be issued by the Department after determining that the applicant is (i) properly licensed, (ii) furnished special surety bonds as required by the Department, and (iii) complying with such other regulations as required by the Department.

(b)   It shall be the duty of the applicant to see that the "beams and dollies" and "hauling units" used shall be constructed with proper material in a suitable manner and utilized so as to provide for the safety of the general public and the structure being relocated. Any violation of this duty may result in suspension or revocation of his license by the Department.

(c)   A license shall not be required for an individual owner of a towing vehicle moving their own buildings from or to property owned individually by those persons; however, a permit will be required for all moves.

(d)   Licensed housemovers shall furnish front and rear certified escort vehicles on all moves, one or both of which may be a marked police, sheriff or State Highway Patrol vehicle as determined by the issuing agent, or one or two properly equipped certified escort vehicles depending on the number of law-enforcement vehicles escorting the move; escort vehicles shall operate where possible at a distance of 300 feet from the structure being moved; that this interval will be closed in cities and other congested areas to protect other traffic from the swing of the load at corners and turns, and the certified escort vehicles shall comply with all restrictions as provided on the permit secured for movement of the structure. (1977, c. 720, s. 5; 1981, c. 818, s. 2; 2005-354, s. 4.)

§ 20-361. Application for permit and permit fee.

Application for a permit to move a structure must be made to the division or district engineer having jurisdiction at least two days prior to the date of the move. For good cause shown, this time may be waived by the district or division engineer. A travel plan and a permit application fee of twenty dollars ($20.00) shall accompany the application. Division or district engineers are authorized to issue permits for individual moves of a structure or building whose width does not exceed 36 feet. The travel plan will show the proposed route, the time estimated for each segment of the move, a plan to handle traffic so that no one delay to other highway users shall exceed 20 minutes. The division or district engineers shall review the travel plan and if the route cannot accommodate the move due to roadway weight limits, bridge size or weight limits, or will cause undue interruption of traffic flow, the permit shall not be issued. The applicant may submit alternate plans if desired until an acceptable route is determined. If the width of the building or structure to be relocated is more than 36 feet, or if no acceptable travel plan has been filed, and the denial of the permit would cause a hardship, the application and travel plan may be submitted to the Department on appeal. After reviewing the route and travel plan, the Department may in its discretion issue the permit after considering the practical physical limitations of the route, the nature and purpose of the move, the size and weight of the structure, the distance the structure is to be moved, and the safety and convenience of the traveling public. A surety bond in an amount to cover the cost of any damage to the pavement, structures, bridges, roadway or other damages that may occur can be required if deemed necessary by the Department. (1977, c. 720, s. 6; 1991 (Reg. Sess., 1992), c. 813, s. 3.)

§ 20-362. Liability of housemovers.

The permittee assumes all responsibility for injury to persons or damage to property of any kind and agrees to hold the Department harmless for any claims arising out of his conduct or actions. (1977, c. 720, s. 7.)

§ 20-363. Removal and replacement of obstructions.

All obstructions, including mailboxes, traffic signals, signs, and utility lines will be removed immediately prior to and replaced immediately after the move at the expense of the mover. Any property, real or personal, to be removed, which is not located in the right-of-way, shall not be removed until the owner is notified and arrangements for and approval from the owner are obtained. (1977, c. 720, s. 8; 2008-89, s. 3.)

§ 20-364. Route changes.

Irrespective of the route shown on the permit, an alternate route will be followed:

(1)   If directed by a peace officer.

(2)   If directed by a uniformed officer assigned to a weigh station to follow a route to a weighing device.

(3)   If the specified route is officially detoured. Should a detour be encountered, the driver shall check with the office issuing permit on which he is traveling prior to proceeding. (1977, c. 720, s. 9; 2004-124, s. 18.3(d).)

§ 20-365. Loading or parking on right-of-way.

The object to be transported will not be loaded, unloaded, nor parked, day or night, on highway right-of-way without specific permission from the district or division engineer. (1977, c. 720, s. 10.)

§ 20-366. Effect of weather.

No move will be made when atmospheric conditions render visibility lower than safe for travel. Moves will not be made when highway is covered with snow or ice, or at any time travel conditions are considered unsafe by the Department or Highway Patrol or other law-enforcement officers having jurisdiction. (1977, c. 720, s. 11.)

§ 20-367. Obtaining license or permit by fraud.

The permit may be voided if any conditions of the permit are violated. Upon any violation, the permit must be surrendered and a new permit obtained before proceeding. Misrepresentation of information on application to obtain a license, fraudulently obtaining a permit, alteration of a permit, or unauthorized use of a permit will render the permit void. (1977, c. 720, s. 12.)

§ 20-368. Municipal regulations.

All moves on streets on the municipal system of streets shall comply with local regulations. (1977, c. 720, s. 13.)

§ 20-369. Out-of-state licenses and permits.

An out-of-state person, partnership, or corporation engaging in the structural moving business may apply to the Department for a license to engage in the housemoving profession in North Carolina, and obtain permits for moves by complying with the provisions of this Article and the regulations of the Department in the same manner as is required of North Carolina residents and by showing that the state in which the housemover operates his business extends similar privileges to housemovers licensed in North Carolina. (1977, c. 720, s. 14; 1979, c. 475, s. 1.)

§ 20-370. Speed limits.

The speed of moves will be that which is reasonable and prudent for the load, considering weight and bulk, under conditions existing at the time. (1977, c. 720, s. 15.)

§ 20-371. Penalties.

(a) Any person violating the provisions of this Article or the regulations of the Department governing housemoving shall be guilty of a Class 1 misdemeanor.

(b) The Department is hereby authorized in the name of the State to apply for relief by injunction, in the established manner provided in cases of civil procedure, without bond, to enforce the provisions of this Article, or to restrain any violation thereof. In such proceedings, it shall not be necessary to allege or prove either that an adequate remedy at law does not exist, or that substantial or irreparable damage would result from the continued violation thereof. (1977, c. 720, s. 16; 1993, c. 539, s. 392; 1994, Ex. Sess., c. 24, s. 14(c); 2008-89, s. 4.)

§ 20-372. Invalid section; severability.

If any of the provisions of this Article, or if the application of such provisions to any person or circumstance shall be held invalid, the remainder of this Article and the application of such provision of this Article other than those as to which it is held valid, shall not be affected thereby. (1977, c. 720, s. 17.)

§ 20-373. Reserved for future codification purposes.

§ 20-374. Unsafe practices.

(a) If the Department determines that a housemover has engaged in unsafe practices, all licenses, permits, and authorizations issued to the person pursuant to this Article shall be revoked for a period of six months.

(b) Any person whose license, permit, or authorization issued under this Article is revoked pursuant to this section may request a hearing to be held before the Secretary or a person designated by the Secretary. The licensee shall be notified in writing no less than 10 days prior to the hearing of the time and place of the hearing. At the hearing, the parties shall be given an opportunity to present evidence on issues of fact, examine and cross-examine witnesses, and present arguments on issues of law. The decision of the Secretary or of the person designated by the Secretary shall be final. Any person aggrieved by the final decision may seek judicial review of the decision in accordance with the provisions of Article 4 of Chapter 150B of the General Statutes. (2008-89, s. 5.)

§ 20-375. Reserved for future codification purposes.

Article 17.

Motor Carrier Safety Regulation Unit.

Part 1. General Provisions.

§ 20-376. Definitions.

The following definitions apply in this Article:

(1) Federal safety and hazardous materials regulations. - The federal motor carrier safety regulations contained in 49 C.F.R. Parts 171 through 180, 382, and 390 through 398.

(2) Foreign commerce. - Commerce between any of the following:

a. A place in the United States and a place in a foreign country.

b. Places in the United States through any foreign country.

(3) Interstate commerce. - As defined in 49 C.F.R. Part 390.5.

(3a) Interstate motor carrier. - Any person, firm, or corporation that operates or controls a commercial motor vehicle as defined in 49 C.F.R. § 390.5 in interstate commerce.

(4) Intrastate commerce. - As defined in 49 C.F.R. Part 390.5.

(5) Intrastate motor carrier. - Any person, firm, or corporation that operates or controls a motor vehicle in intrastate commerce when the vehicle:

a. Is a vehicle having a gross vehicle weight rating (GVWR) or gross combination weight rating (GCWR) or gross vehicle weight (GVW) or gross combination weight (GCW) of 26,001 pounds or more, whichever is greater.

b. Is designed or used to transport 16 or more passengers, including the driver.

c. Is used in transporting a hazardous material in a quantity requiring placarding pursuant to 49 C.F.R. Parts 170 through 185. (1985, c. 454, s. 1; 1993 (Reg. Sess., 1994), c. 621, s. 5; 1995 (Reg. Sess., 1996), c. 756, s. 20; 1997-456, s. 36; 1998-149, s. 11; 1999-452, s. 21; 2002-152, s. 3; 2010-129, s. 5.)

Part 2. Authority and Powers of Department of Public Safety.

§ 20-377. General powers of Department of Public Safety.

The Department of Public Safety shall have and exercise such general power and authority to supervise and control the motor carriers of the State as may be necessary to carry out the laws providing for their regulation, and all such other powers and duties as may be necessary or incident to the proper discharge of its duties. (1985, c. 454, s. 1; 2002-159, s. 31.5(b); 2002-190, s. 2; 2011-145, s. 19.1(g).)

§ 20-378: Repealed by Session Laws 1995 (Regular Session, 1996), c. 756, s. 21.

§ 20-379. Department of Public Safety to audit motor carriers for compliance.

The Department of Public Safety must periodically audit each motor carrier to determine if the carrier is complying with this Article and, if the motor carrier is subject to regulation by the North Carolina Utilities Commission, with Chapter 62 of the General Statutes. In conducting the audit, the Department of Public Safety may examine a person under oath, compel the production of papers and the attendance of witnesses, and copy a paper for use in the audit. An employee of the Department of Public Safety may enter the premises of a motor carrier during reasonable hours to enforce this Article. When on the premises of a motor carrier, an employee of the Department of Public Safety may set up and use equipment needed to make the tests required by this Article. (1985, c. 454, s. 1; 1995 (Reg. Sess., 1996), c. 756, s. 22; 2002-159, s. 31.5(b); 2002-190, s. 2; 2011-145, s. 19.1(g).)

§ 20-380. Department of Public Safety may investigate accidents involving motor carriers and promote general safety program.

The Department of Public Safety may conduct a program of accident prevention and public safety covering all motor carriers with special emphasis on highway safety and transport safety and may investigate the causes of any accident on a highway involving a motor carrier. Any information obtained in an investigation shall be reduced to writing and a report thereof filed in the office of the Department of Public Safety, which shall be subject to public inspection but such report shall not be admissible in evidence in any civil or criminal proceeding arising from such accident. The Department of Public Safety may adopt rules for the safety of the public as affected by motor carriers and the safety of motor carrier employees. The Department of Public Safety shall cooperate with and coordinate its activities for motor carriers with other agencies and organizations engaged in the promotion of highway safety and employee safety. (1985, c. 454, s. 1; 1995 (Reg. Sess., 1996), c. 756, s. 23; 2002-159, s. 31.5(b); 2002-190, s. 2; 2011-145, s. 19.1(g).)

§ 20-381. Specific powers and duties of Department of Public Safety applicable to motor carriers; agricultural exemption.

(a) The Department of Public Safety has the following powers and duties concerning motor carriers:

(1) To prescribe qualifications and maximum hours of service of drivers and their helpers.

(1a) To set safety standards for vehicles of motor carriers engaged in foreign, interstate, or intrastate commerce over the highways of this State and for the safe operation of these vehicles. The Department of Public Safety may stop, enter upon, and perform inspections of motor carriers' vehicles in operation to determine compliance with these standards and may conduct any investigations and tests it finds necessary to promote the safety of equipment and the safe operation on the highway of these vehicles.

(1b) To enforce this Article, rules adopted under this Article, and the federal safety and hazardous materials regulations.

(2) To enter the premises of a motor carrier to inspect a motor vehicle or any equipment used by the motor carrier in transporting passengers or property.

(2a) To prohibit the use by a motor carrier of any motor vehicle or motor vehicle equipment the Department of Public Safety finds, by reason of its mechanical condition or loading, would be likely to cause a crash or breakdown in the transportation of passengers or property on a highway. If an agent of the Department of Public Safety finds a motor vehicle of a motor carrier in actual use upon the highways in the transportation of passengers or property that, by reason of its mechanical condition or loading, would be likely to cause a crash or breakdown, the agent shall declare the vehicle "Out of Service." The agent shall require the operator thereof to discontinue its use and to substitute therefor a safe vehicle, parts or equipment at the earliest possible time and place, having regard for both the convenience and the safety of the passengers or property. When an inspector or agent stops a motor vehicle on the highway, under authority of this section, and the motor vehicle is declared "Out of Service," no motor carrier operator shall require, or permit, any person to operate, nor shall any person operate, any motor vehicle equipment declared "Out of Service" until all repairs required by the "Out of Service" notice have been satisfactorily completed. Such agents or inspectors shall also have the right to stop any motor vehicle which is being used upon the public highways for the transportation of passengers or property by a motor carrier subject to the provisions of this Article and to eject therefrom any driver or operator who shall be operating or be in charge of such motor vehicle while under the influence of alcoholic beverages or impairing substances. It shall be the duty of all inspectors and agents of the Department of Public Safety to make a written report, upon a form prescribed by the Department of Public Safety, of inspections of all motor equipment and a copy of each such written report, disclosing defects in such equipment, shall be served promptly upon the motor carrier operating the same, either in person by the inspector or agent or by mail. Such agents and inspectors shall also make and serve a similar written report in cases where a motor vehicle is operated in violation of this Chapter or, if the motor vehicle is subject to regulation by the North Carolina Utilities Commission, of Chapter 62 of the General Statutes.

(3)   To relieve the highways of all undue burdens and safeguard traffic thereon by adopting and enforcing rules and orders designed and calculated to minimize the dangers attending transportation on the highways of all hazardous materials and other commodities.

(4)   To determine the safety fitness of intrastate motor carriers, to assign safety ratings to intrastate motor carriers as defined in 49 C.F.R. § 385.3, to direct intrastate motor carriers to take remedial action when required, to prohibit the operation of intrastate motor carriers rated unsatisfactory, to determine whether the continued operations of intrastate motor carriers pose an "imminent hazard" as defined in 49 C.F.R. § 386.72(b)(1), and to prohibit the operation of an intrastate motor carrier found to be an "imminent hazard" as defined in 49 C.F.R. § 386.72(b)(1).

(5)   To prohibit the intrastate operation of a motor carrier subject to an order issued by the Federal Motor Carrier Safety Administration to cease all operations based on a finding that the continued operations of the motor carrier pose an "imminent hazard" as defined in 49 C.F.R. § 386.72(b)(1).

(b)   The definitions set out in 49 Code of Federal Regulations § 171.8 apply to this subsection. The transportation of an agricultural product, other than a Class 2 material, over local roads between fields of the same farm by a farmer operating as an intrastate private motor carrier is exempt from the requirements of Parts 171 through 180 of 49 CFR as provided in 49 CFR § 173.5(a). The transportation of an agricultural product to or from a farm within 150 miles of the farm by a farmer operating as an intrastate private motor carrier is exempt from the requirements of Subparts G and H of Part 172 of 49 CFR as provided in 49

CFR § 173.5(b). (1985, c. 454, s. 1; 1995 (Reg. Sess., 1996), c. 756, s. 24; 1997-456, ss. 37, 38; 1998-149, s. 12; 1998-165, s. 1; 1999-452, s. 22; 2002-152, ss. 4, 5; 2002-159, s. 31.5(b); 2002-190, s. 2; 2009-376, s. 9; 2011-145, s. 19.1(g).)

§ 20-382. For-hire motor carrier registration, insurance verification, and temporary trip permit authority.

(a) UCRA. - The Commissioner may enter into the Unified Carrier Registration Agreement (UCRA), established pursuant to Section 4305 of Public Law 109-73, and into agreements with jurisdictions participating in the UCRA to exchange information for any audit or enforcement activity required by the UCRA. Upon entry into the UCRA, the requirements set under the UCRA apply to the Division. If a requirement set under the UCRA conflicts with this section, the UCRA controls. Rules adopted to implement this section must ensure compliance with mandates of the Federal Motor Carrier Safety Administration and the United States Department of Transportation.

(a1) Carrier Registration. - A motor carrier may not operate a for-hire motor vehicle in interstate commerce in this State unless the motor carrier has complied with all of the following requirements:

(1) Registered its operations with its base state.

(1a) Done one of the following:

a. Filed a copy of the certificate of authority issued to it by the United States Department of Transportation allowing it to transport regulated items in this State and any amendments to that authority.

b. Certified to the Division that it carries only items that are not regulated by the United States Department of Transportation.

(2) Verified, in accordance with subsection (b) of this section, that it has insurance for each for-hire motor vehicle it operates.

(3) Paid the fees set in G.S. 20-385.

(b) Insurance Verification. - A motor carrier that operates a for-hire motor vehicle in interstate commerce in this State and is regulated by the United States Department of Transportation must verify to the Division that each for-hire motor vehicle the motor carrier operates in this State is insured in accordance with the requirements set by the United States Department of Transportation. A motor carrier that operates a for-hire motor vehicle in interstate commerce in this State and is exempt from regulation by the United States Department of Transportation must verify to the Division that each for-hire motor vehicle the motor carrier operates in this State is insured in accordance with the requirements set by the North Carolina Utilities Commission.

(c) Trip Permit. - A motor carrier that is not registered as required by this section may obtain an emergency trip permit. An emergency trip permit allows the motor carrier to operate a for-hire motor vehicle in this State for a period not to exceed 10 days. (1985, c. 454, s. 1; 1993 (Reg. Sess., 1994), c. 621, s. 1; 1995 (Reg. Sess., 1996), c. 756, s. 25; 2007-492, s. 3; 2010-97, s. 4.)

§ 20-382.1. Registration of for-hire intrastate motor carriers and verification that their vehicles are insured.

(a) Registration. - A for-hire motor carrier may not operate a for-hire motor vehicle in intrastate commerce in this State unless the motor carrier has complied with all of the following requirements:

(1) For a motor carrier that hauls household goods, registered its operations with the State by doing one of the following:

a. Obtaining a certificate of authority from the North Carolina Utilities Commission.

b. Obtaining a certificate of exemption from the Division.

(1a) For a motor carrier that does not haul household goods, registered its operations with the Division.

(2) Verified, in accordance with subsection (b) of this section, that it has insurance for each for-hire motor vehicle it operates in this State.

(3) Paid the fees set in G.S. 20-385.

(b) Insurance Verification. - A for-hire motor carrier that operates a for-hire vehicle in intrastate commerce in this State must verify to the Division that each for-hire motor vehicle it operates in this State is insured. To do this, the motor carrier must submit an insurance verification form to the Division and must file annually with the Division a list of the for-hire vehicles it operates in this State. (1993 (Reg. Sess., 1994), c. 621, s. 2; 1995 (Reg. Sess., 1996), c. 756, s. 26.)

§ 20-382.2. Penalty for failure to comply with registration or insurance verification requirements.

(a) Acts. - A motor carrier who does any of the following is subject to a civil penalty of one thousand dollars ($1,000):

(1) Operates a for-hire motor vehicle in this State without registering its operations, as required by this Part.

(2) Repealed by Session Laws 2007-492, s. 4, effective August 30, 2007.

(3) Operates a for-hire motor vehicle in intrastate commerce in this State for which it has not verified it has insurance, as required by G.S. 20-382.1.

(b) Payment and Review. - When the Department of Public Safety finds that a for-hire motor vehicle is operated in this State in violation of the registration and insurance verification requirements of this Part, the Department must place the motor vehicle out of service until the motor carrier is in compliance and the penalty imposed under this section is paid unless the officer that imposes the penalty determines that operation of the motor vehicle will not jeopardize collection of the penalty. A motor carrier that denies liability for a penalty imposed under this section may pay the penalty under protest and follow the procedure in G.S. 20-178.1 for a departmental review of the penalty.

(c) Judicial Restriction. - A court of this State may not issue a restraining order or an injunction to restrain or enjoin the collection of a penalty imposed under this section or to permit the operation of a vehicle placed out of service under this section without payment of the penalty.

(d) Proceeds. - A penalty imposed under this section is payable to the Department of Transportation, Fiscal Section. The clear proceeds of all civil penalties assessed by the Department pursuant to this section, minus any fees paid as interest, filing fees, attorneys' fees, or other necessary costs of court associated with the defense of penalties imposed pursuant to this section shall be remitted to the Civil Penalty and Forfeiture Fund in accordance with G.S. 115C-457.2. (1993 (Reg. Sess., 1994), c. 621, s. 3; 1997-466, s. 3; 2002-159, s. 31.5(b); 2002-190, ss. 2, 3; 2005-64, s. 1; 2007-492, s. 4; 2009-376, ss. 2(b), 14; 2011-145, s. 19.1(g).)

§ 20-383. Inspectors and officers given enforcement authority.

Only designated inspectors, officers, and personnel of the Department of Public Safety shall have the authority to enforce the provisions of this Article and provisions of Chapter 62 applicable to motor transportation, and they are empowered to make complaint for the issue of appropriate warrants, information, presentments or other lawful process for the enforcement and prosecution of violations of the transportation laws against all offenders, whether they be regulated motor carriers or not, and to appear in court or before the North Carolina Utilities Commission and offer evidence at the trial pursuant to such processes. (1985, c. 454, s. 1; 2002-159, s. 31.5(b); 2002-190, s. 2; 2011-145, s. 19.1(g); 2012-78, s. 10.)

§ 20-384. Penalty for certain violations.

A motor carrier who fails to conduct a safety inspection of a vehicle as required by Part 396 of the federal safety regulations or who fails to mark a vehicle that has been inspected as required by that Part commits an infraction and, if found responsible, is liable for a penalty of up to fifty dollars ($50.00). (1985, c. 454, s. 1; 1985 (Reg. Sess., 1986), c. 1018, s. 13; 1993 (Reg. Sess., 1994), c. 754, s. 6; 1995 (Reg. Sess., 1996), c. 756, s. 27.)

Part 3. Fees and Charges.

§ 20-385. Fee schedule.

(a) The fees listed in this section apply to a motor carrier. These fees are in addition to any fees required under the Unified Carrier Registration Agreement.

(1) Repealed by Session Laws 2007-492, s. 5, effective August 30, 2007.

(2) Application by an intrastate motor carrier for a

certificate of exemption
45.00

(3) Certification by an interstate motor carrier that it is

not regulated by the United States Department

of Transportation
45.00

(4) Application by an interstate motor carrier for an

emergency trip permit
18.00.

(b) Repealed by Session Laws 2007-492, s. 5, effective August 30, 2007. (1985, c. 454, s. 1; 1993 (Reg. Sess., 1994), c. 621, s. 4; 1995 (Reg. Sess., 1996), c. 756, s. 28; 2005-276, s. 44.1(p); 2007-492, s. 5.)

§ 20-386. Fees, charges and penalties; disposition.

All fees and charges received by the Division under G.S. 20-385 shall be in addition to any other tax or fee provided by law and shall be placed in the Highway Fund. (1985, c. 454, s. 1.)

Part 4. Penalties and Actions.

§ 20-387. Motor carrier violating any provision of Article, rules or orders; penalty.

Any motor carrier which violates any of the provisions of this Article or refuses to conform to or obey any rule, order or regulation of the Division or Department of Public Safety shall, in addition to the other penalties prescribed in this Article forfeit and pay a sum up to one thousand dollars ($1,000) for each offense, to be recovered in an action to be instituted in the Superior Court of Wake County, in the name of the State of North Carolina on the relation of the Department of Public Safety; and each day such motor carrier continues to violate any provision of this Article or continues to refuse to obey or perform any rule, order or regulation prescribed by the Division or Department of Public Safety shall be a separate offense. (1985, c. 454, s. 1; 2002-159, s. 31.5(b); 2002-159, s. 31.5(b); 2002-190, s. 10; 2011-145, s. 19.1(g).)

§ 20-388. Willful acts of employees deemed those of motor carrier.

The willful act of any officer, agent, or employee of a motor carrier, acting within the scope of his official duties of employment, shall, for the purpose of this Article, be deemed to be the willful act of the motor carrier. (1985, c. 454, s. 1.)

§ 20-389. Actions to recover penalties.

Except as otherwise provided in this Article, an action for the recovery of any penalty under this Article shall be instituted in Wake County, and shall be instituted in the name of the State of North Carolina on the relation of the Department of Public Safety against the person incurring such penalty; or whenever such action is upon the complaint of any injured person, it shall be instituted in the name of the State of North Carolina on the relation of the Department of Public Safety upon the complaint of such injured person against the person incurring such penalty. Such action may be instituted and prosecuted by the Attorney General, the District Attorney of the Wake County Superior Court, or the injured person. The procedure in such actions, the right of appeal and the rules regulating appeals shall be the same as provided by law in other civil actions. (1985, c. 454, s. 1; 2002-159, s. 31.5(b); 2002-190, s. 2; 2011-145, s. 19.1(g).)

§ 20-390. Refusal to permit Department of Public Safety to inspect records made misdemeanor.

Any motor carrier, its officers or agents in charge thereof, that fails or refuses upon the written demand of the Department of Public Safety to permit its authorized representatives or employees to examine and inspect its books, records, accounts and documents, or its plant, property, or facilities, as provided for by law, shall be guilty of a Class 3 misdemeanor. Each day of such failure or refusal shall constitute a separate offense and each such offense shall be punishable only by a fine of not less than five hundred dollars ($500.00) and not more than five thousand dollars ($5,000). (1985, c. 454, s. 1; 1993, c. 539, s. 393; 1994, Ex. Sess., c. 24, s. 14(c); 2002-159, s. 31.5(b); 2002-190, s. 2; 2011-145, s. 19.1(g).)

§ 20-391. Violating rules, with injury to others.

If any motor carrier doing business in this State by its agents or employees shall be guilty of the violations of the rules and regulations provided and prescribed by the Division or the Department of Public Safety, and if after due notice of such violation given to the principal officer thereof, if residing in the State, or, if not, to the manager or superintendent or secretary or treasurer if residing in the State, or, if not, then to any local agent thereof, ample and full recompense for the wrong or injury done thereby to any person as may be directed by the Division or Department of Public Safety shall not be made within 30 days from the time of such notice, such motor carrier shall incur a penalty for each offense of five hundred dollars ($500.00). (1985, c. 454, s. 1; 2002-159, s. 31.5(b); 2002-190, s. 11; 2011-145, s. 19.1(g).)

§ 20-392. Failure to make report; obstructing Division or Department of Public Safety.

Every officer, agent or employee of any motor carrier, who shall willfully neglect or refuse to make and furnish any report required by the Division or Department of Public Safety for the purposes of this Article, or who shall willfully or unlawfully hinder, delay or obstruct the Division or Department of Public Safety in the discharge of the duties hereby imposed upon it, shall forfeit and pay five hundred dollars ($500.00) for each offense, to be recovered in an action in the name of the State. A delay of 10 days to make and furnish such report shall raise the presumption that the same was willful. (1985, c. 454, s. 1; 2002-159, s. 31.5(b); 2002-190, s. 12; 2011-145, s. 19.1(g).)

§ 20-393. Disclosure of information by employee of Department of Public Safety unlawful.

It shall be unlawful for any agent or employee of the Department of Public Safety knowingly and willfully to divulge any fact or information which may come to his knowledge during the course of any examination or inspection made under authority of this Article, except to the Department of Public Safety or as may be directed by the Department of Public Safety or upon approval of a request to the Department of Public Safety by the Utilities Commission or by a court or judge thereof. (1985, c. 454, s. 1; 2002-159, s. 31.5(b); 2002-190, s. 2; 2011-145, s. 19.1(g).)

§ 20-394. Remedies for injuries cumulative.

The remedies given by this Article to persons injured shall be regarded as cumulative to the remedies otherwise provided by law against motor carriers. (1985, c. 454, s. 1.)

§ 20-395. Willful injury to property of motor carrier a misdemeanor.

If any person shall willfully do or cause to be done any act or acts whatever whereby any building, construction or work of any motor carrier, or any engine, machine or structure of any matter or thing appertaining to the same shall be stopped, obstructed, impaired, weakened, injured or destroyed, he shall be guilty of a Class 1 misdemeanor. (1985, c. 454, s. 1; 1993, c. 539, s. 394; 1994, Ex. Sess., c. 24, s. 14(c).)

§ 20-396. Unlawful motor carrier operations.

(a) Any person, whether carrier, shipper, consignee, or any officer, employee, agent, or representative thereof, who by means of any false statement or representation, or by the use of any false or fictitious bill, bill of lading, receipt, voucher, roll, account, claim, certificate, affidavit, deposition, lease, or bill of sale, or by any other means or device, shall knowingly and willfully seek to evade or defeat regulations as in this Article provided for motor carriers, shall be deemed guilty of a Class 3 misdemeanor and only punished by a fine of not more than five hundred dollars ($500.00) for the first offense and not more than two thousand dollars ($2,000) for any subsequent offense.

(b) Any motor carrier, or other person, or any officer, agent, employee, or representative thereof, who shall willfully fail or refuse to make a report to the Division or Department of Public Safety as required by this Article, or other applicable law, or to make specific and full, true, and correct answer to any question within 30 days from the time it is lawfully required by the Division or Department of Public Safety so to do, or to keep accounts, records, and memoranda in the form and manner prescribed by the Division or Department of Public Safety or shall knowingly and willfully falsify, destroy, mutilate, or alter any such report, account, record, or memorandum, or shall knowingly and willfully neglect or fail to make true and correct entries in such accounts, records, or memoranda of all facts and transactions appertaining to the business of the carrier, or person required under this Article to keep the same, or shall knowingly and willfully keep any accounts, records, or memoranda contrary to the rules, regulations, or orders of the Division or Department of Public Safety with respect thereto, shall be deemed guilty of a Class 3 misdemeanor and be punished for each offense only by a fine of not more than five thousand dollars ($5,000). As used in this subsection the words "kept" and "keep" shall be construed to mean made, prepared or compiled as well as retained. (1985, c. 454, s. 1; 1993, c. 539, s. 395; 1994, Ex. Sess., c. 24, s. 14(c); 2002-159, s. 31.5(b); 2002-190, s. 13; 2011-145, s. 19.1(g).)

§ 20-397. Furnishing false information to the Department of Public Safety; withholding information from the Department of Public Safety.

(a) Every person, firm or corporation operating under the jurisdiction of the Department of Public Safety or who is required by law to file reports with the Department of Public Safety who shall knowingly or willfully file or give false information to the Department of Public Safety in any report, reply, response, or other statement or document furnished to the Department of Public Safety shall be guilty of a Class 1 misdemeanor.

(b) Every person, firm, or corporation operating under the jurisdiction of the Department of Public Safety or who is required by law to file reports with the Department of Public Safety who shall willfully withhold clearly specified and reasonably obtainable information from the Department of Public Safety in any report, response, reply or statement filed with the Department of Public Safety in the performance of the duties of the Department of Public Safety or who shall fail or refuse to file any report, response, reply or statement required by the Department of Public Safety in the performance of the duties of the Department of Public Safety shall be guilty of a Class 1 misdemeanor. (1985, c. 454, s. 1; 1993, c. 539, s. 396; 1994, Ex. Sess., c. 24, s. 14(c); 2002-159, s. 31.5(b); 2002-190, s. 2; 2011-145, s. 19.1(g).)

§ 20-398. Household goods carrier; marking or identification of vehicles.

(a) No carrier shall operate any motor vehicle upon a highway, public street, or public vehicular area within the State in the transportation of household goods for compensation unless the name or trade name and the North Carolina number assigned to the carrier by the North Carolina Utilities Commission appear on each side of the vehicle in letters and figures not less than three inches high. The North Carolina number assigned to the carrier shall also be placed on the rear left upper quadrant of the vehicle in letters and figures not less than three inches high. In case of a tractor-trailer unit, the side markings must be on the tractor and the rear markings must be on the trailer. The markings required may be printed on the vehicle or on durable placards securely fastened on the vehicle.

(b) Except as provided in subsection (b) of this section, the provisions of this section shall apply to every vehicle used by the carrier in his or her operation whether owned, rented, leased, or otherwise. However, if a vehicle is rented or leased, the words "Operated By" shall also appear above or preceding the name of the carrier, unless the vehicles are under permanent lease, in which case the name of the lessor and the words "Operated By" need not appear.

(c) The provisions of this section do not apply to carriers engaged only in interstate commerce. If the carrier is engaged in both interstate and intrastate commerce and is marked as required by the Federal Motor Carrier Safety

Administration, then in that case, it will only be necessary for the carrier to print his or her North Carolina number in a conspicuous place near his or her name in letters and figures corresponding in size with Federal Motor Carrier Safety Administration regulations.

(d)   Any person, whether carrier or any officer, employee, agent, or representative thereof, who violates this section shall be guilty of a Class 3 misdemeanor and punished only by a fine of not more than five hundred dollars ($500.00) for the first offense and not more than two thousand dollars ($2,000) for any subsequent offense. (2011-244, s. 1.)

Vision Books Order Form

Fax Orders:	1-980-299-5965
Phone Orders:	1-704-898-0770
E-mail Orders:	www.visionbooks.org
Mail Orders:	Vision Books, LLC P.O. Box 42406 Charlotte, NC 28215

Shipp To:
Name_____
Address_____
City_____State_____Zip_____
Phone_____Fax_____
Email_____@_____

Bill To: We can bill a third party on your behalf.
Name_____
Address_____
City_____State_____Zip_____
Phone____(_____)_____Fax_____
Email_____@_____

Pamphlet Number ($15.00 Each)	Qty	Total Cost
_____	_____	_____
_____	_____	_____
_____	_____	_____
_____	_____	_____
_____	_____	_____
_____	_____	_____
_____	_____	_____
_____	_____	_____
Full Volume Set 1-92	92 Pamphlets	1,380.00

Free Shipping Shipping & Handling on Full Volume Orders
Add $1.00 Shipping & Handling per pamphlet $_____

Total Cost $_____

<u>Thank You for Your Support. Management!</u>

DID YOU ENJOY THIS BOOK?

Vision Books would like to hear from you! If you or someone you know has been falsely imprisoned, we would like to hear your story. If the 'North Carolina Criminal Law and Procedure' has had an effect in your life or if you have suggestions, we would like to hear from you. Send your letters to:

Vision Books, LLC
Attn: Staff Writers
P.O. Box 42406
Charlotte, NC 28215
Email: staff@visionbooks.org

Order Additional Copies:

Fax Orders: 1-980-299-5965

Phone Orders: 1-704-898-0770

E-mail Orders: www.visionbooks.org

Mail Orders: Vision Books, LLC
                       P.O. Box 42406
                       Charlotte, NC 28215

www.ingramcontent.com/pod-product-compliance
Lightning Source LLC
Chambersburg PA
CBHW051526170526
45165CB00002B/625